DIGITAL PRIVACY

INTERNET SECURITY TO STOP BIG COMPANIES FROM TRACKING AND SELLING YOUR DATA

ERIC FASTER

CHRIS CAPRA

DIGITAL PRIVACY

CONTENTS

Introduction to Privacy   ix

1. AVOID THE BIG BOYS   1
   Google   2
   Amazon   4
   Facebook   7
   Apple   10
   Microsoft   11

2. SOCIAL MEDIA PITFALLS   13
   Facebook   14
   Twitter   17
   Reddit   19
   Options to Stay Safe on Social Media   20

3. HARDWARE TO CONSIDER   22
   The Snowden Laptop   22
   Keeping Your Phone Safe   24
   Picking a Router   25
   Other Dangers to be Careful with   26
   Modem   29
   Raspberry Pi   29
   NextCloud   30

4. SOFTWARE TO CONSIDER   32
   Choosing Your Operating System   32
   Windows   33
   Mac OS   33
   Linux   34
   Mobile Operating Systems   34
   Android   35
   iOS   36

Linux   36
The Security Software You Need   37
Malware Protection   37
Virus Detector   38
VPN   39
Password Managers   40
Browsing Safely Online   41
The Best Browsers to Use   42
Picking the Right Settings   43
Extensions That Can Help You   44
How to Spot Dangerous Extensions   45
Protecting Your Email   46
The Best Secure Email Services   47
What is Disposable Email?   48
The Worst Email Servers   49
How Maps Are Harming Your Security   50
The Good and the Bad of Cloud Storage   50
Shopping Safely Online   52
Local with Cash is King   53
Why Amazon is Good for Online Shopping   54
Things to Consider with Shipping   55
Why Store Memberships Are Bad   57
The CVS Story   58
Delete Me, Please   59

5. BANKING   60
Which Is Better: Credit Union or Big Banks?   60
Credit Cards Selling Data   61
Using a Burner Card from Privacy.com   63
The Argument for Not Card Cutting   65
Is PayPal Safe?   65
Should I Use Bitcoin?   67

6. SEARCH ENGINES   69
DuckDuckGo   69
Startpage   70
Ixquick   71

Blekko   71
Google, Bing, and More   71

7. DIY PROJECTS   73
How to Set Up a Personal Cloud   73
Raspberry Pi   75
Pi-Hole to Block Ads and Malicious Sites   76
Set Up a Private DNS Service   78
Securing a Router   78
What Model to Buy   79
How to Set Up Your VPN Router   81
Considering Anonabox   82

8. LAN/DEVICE CONFIGURATION   84
No SSID Broadcast   85
Turn the Locations Off Your Devices   86
How DNS Can Keep Us Safe   87
Router Settings to Keep You Safe   89
Automatic Updates   89
Set Up Some Stronger Encryption   90
Build in a Firewall   90
Optimized Quad9 DNS Settings   91
Don't Allow for Remote Access   92

9. BEST PRACTICES   93
Consider: Do I Really Need the Product or   93
Service?
How to Turn Off Data Sharing   94
Google   94
Facebook   95
Twitter   96
Shopping Local and with Cash   97
Use the Burner Credit Cards   97
Consider Two-Factor Authentication   98
Different Passwords on All Accounts   99
Never Store Your Cards with Online Accounts   100
Avoid the Rewards Programs   100
Get Everyone on the Same Page   101

10. Final Thoughts   103

References & Links   105

Congratulations and thanks for purchasing *Digital Privacy: Internet Security to Stop Big Companies from Tracking and Selling Your Data*. You've just taken the very first step toward protecting your online privacy and security.

Upon writing this book, our intent is to inform you of all the ways in which companies and governments can attempt to track and sell your data.

At the time of publication, we made our best effort to ensure that all information in this book is current and accurate. Because of the technical nature of the content, and the reality of fast-moving technologies, it is highly likely that portions of the content will become outdated at some point. However, some of the strategies and best practices will remain valid no matter which technology is implemented. Please keep this in mind while you're building your own digital privacy and security plan.

In the following chapters, we will discuss digital privacy and what it means, how things have changed, and what is happening online in this new digital world. We will also discuss what your options are, and I'll show you some concrete steps that you can take to protect yourself and your family. By reading this book, you've started down the road to learning all about internet security, privacy, and anonymity. So, pour yourself a stiff drink, settle into your favorite easy chair, and let's get started.

THE PROBLEM TODAY

Let's start with the harsh truth that you need to know right up front: YOU are being sold. I know that sounds confusing, but hear me out. By you, I mean your data. Your online life. All of it is collected, compiled, packaged and sold to the highest bidder. You ARE the product.

Have you ever noticed that everything is free? Twitter is free. Gmail is free. Facebook, Instagram, and Pinterest. Just name any social network. They are all free to use. Yet, somehow, they report mega-profits into the billions of dollars, year after year.

How is that possible? You're probably thinking: Where does the money come from? All these companies have zero products to sell. Well, I'm here to tell you, that's not exactly true. They have you. That's correct. You are the product. And what a product! In 2016, personal data surpassed oil to become the single most valuable asset for sale worldwide, and yours is being sold, too. Shivon Zilis, a project director for Bloomberg Beta, said, "Data is the new oil," when commenting on its rapidly increasing value.

Have you ever merely thought about something, and then it shows up in your Facebook feed? Ever thought about a new product, and then started seeing ads for that exact same product? No, you're not going crazy. That is really happening—and in this book, we'll discuss how.

What you are experiencing is data-profiling on steroids. And yes, companies have been doing some version of it since the beginning of commerce. Long ago, retailers have gone on record saying their data can accurately determine what you will buy next based on markers from what you've bought previously. But what is happening today is on a whole new level and is almost unbelievable.

Right now, hundreds of companies have created a personal dossier that consists of everything about you, including your likes and dislikes, things you buy, places you shop and visit, banks and credit cards you use, hobbies and interests, political affiliations and whether you are likely to vote, your health records, your citizenship status, your gender preferences, which constitutional amendments you support, among other things. That's not all of it, and the list goes on. I just got tired of typing. There's even more that they know about you. Tons more.

One of the ways they can use this data against you is price discrimination. You might be asking yourself, price what? Well, it is exactly what it sounds like. You get a different online price than your neighbor for the same product or service. If you're angry about that, maybe you should be. But, don't hold your breath waiting for things to change. If anything, this type of strategy will only increase in the future.

Here's how it works. The online retailer keeps a data history all about you. They know your gender, your purchasing history, whether or not you shop around for the lowest price, your location, and many other factors. They use this information against you to set a custom price that maximizes their profit. It's a form of one-way haggling, where the store gets to try out different prices, but you don't get to negotiate in return. Fun!

For all of history, retailers have only had one price option for everyone. This, of course, was not ideal for them. They may have missed out on customers who were willing to pay much more for the product. Adversely, they also missed out on customers who walked away without buying but would have bought if a small discount was offered.

Those days are over. Now, online retailers have a distinct advantage and can optimize their pricing for each customer. And they are doing it.

In one test, Expedia offered different hotel rates depending on who was searching, what their history was, their location, and even which device they were on. Some got lower prices when searching with a cell phone vs. their laptop. Some did better when using an incognito private browser vs. their regular browser.

When confronted with these test results, and the accusation of price discrimination, the vice president of Expedia responded, "Our customers tell us, it's awesome!"

Another example of misuse of your data is election influence. Facebook performed an experiment during the 2010 election (which they didn't tell anyone about) and published the results two years later. It involved 60 million Facebook users who were sent a "go vote" reminder. This influenced an additional 360,000 people to get off the couch and vote. These were people who otherwise would not have voted. Can you see what can happen next? Companies can literally control exactly who goes to vote. When that's Facebook, which almost 7 in 10 US voting adults use, companies can control democratic elections.

That's just the meager beginning.

This data mining technique was perfected just in time for the 2016 election when a British company called Cambridge

Analytica demonstrated its real power. The company claimed to have over 500 data points on every single American. EVERY. SINGLE. AMERICAN. But they didn't need to use all of it. They used a technique made famous by emergency nurses called triage in which voters were organized into three groups. Those who will definitely vote. Those who will never vote. And the third, and most important group, those who might vote, but only if prompted to do so. This third group is who they focused on. But they didn't need all those people. They only needed to reach the ones who were more likely to vote for Trump. And even then, they didn't even need all of those individuals. They only needed to reach those people located in very specific voting districts where Trump's support was weak. Just enough people to win. Cambridge Analytica sent messages, election propaganda and "go vote" reminders to those people. It worked better than expected and even shocked well-known political analysts when Trump actually won.

There may be even more insidious misuses of your data for political purposes. These are the deeds we can't know about but can only imagine. And if we can imagine them, then chances are they are already in use.

Here's a thought experiment. Imagine you attempt to help your community, and you decide to run for office. I know. You have no political ambitions, but just bear with me. The constituents seem to like you, and your campaign is gaining traction. Then, a potential big donor wants to meet you for lunch and talk to you about the campaign. He arrives with an envelope and presents it to you. It contains your health records showing you had a history of mental health problems as a teen. It also has proof of exposing your close friend as an undocumented alien. There are also nude photos that your spouse shared privately with you. He makes it clear that the photos will be released on the internet, Immigrations and Customs Enforcement (ICE) will be notified about your close friend's location, and your health records will be leaked. All he is asking is that you quietly exit the election race. He and his powerful friends have another candidate in mind. Or worse! They make you win the elected office and then control your political decisions until you retire—when they choose for you to do so.

There is no way to know how many times something like that has already happened, but I bet it's more than you think. It's yet another way data brokers can influence an election, and nobody would ever know. Especially if these candidates were approached before they even got started. In the example above, none of those things you did were illegal. But because your privacy was violated, you were left vulnerable to manipulation.

You might decide that it's no big deal. I have nothing to hide. If that's your attitude, I ask you to reconsider.

The truth is, everyone has something to hide. Yep, even you. If you think you don't, my email address will be at the back of this book. Please consider sending me all your passwords, all your bank accounts, and full access to your emails, texts, photos, sales receipts, health records, citizenship status, taxes, and social media accounts.

Just the process of imagining me with all that data probably jogged your memory and reminded you that there is something personal you'd prefer I didn't know. However, even if you happen to be that one magical unicorn who is completely without sin, arguing against privacy is flawed thinking.

Surrendering your right to privacy because you "have nothing to hide" is a little bit like saying you don't believe in free speech because you have nothing to say. Or that you don't believe in the right to vote because you don't care who wins. When I think about it, a more accurate analogy would be: you don't care about women's right to vote, because you trust the male politicians to do the right thing. Doesn't sound like a great argument, does it? It's not.

But in the digital data world, it seems like our only option is to trust that the companies will do the right thing.

OUR GOALS

So, what should we do? That is a great question. The goal of this book is to make you aware of the problem and to give you some possible solutions. With that in mind, we'll try to attack three distinct goals.

1. Security

We'll try to give you the best possible advice to help you traverse the internet safely and anonymously, without nefarious corporate spy cams watching your every digital move. Some of the techniques we discuss will also make your online presence more secure and help you avoid getting hacked by malicious criminals.

2. Convenience

A key part of the internet is convenience. In fact, that's one of the best things about it. So, our plan should include ways to minimize impacts to your digital lifestyle. Hopefully, we can achieve that goal and create an environment that lets you operate on the web the way you always have—well, kind of.

3. Privacy

The third, and maybe most important goal, is to help you avoid having your online activity tracked, logged and sold. For this, we'll need to block some services on your computer. Some of these blocks may break your internet experience, thus violating the second goal (convenience). We'll explain which ones and how they work, so you can make some choices you're comfortable with.

BASIC ASSUMPTIONS

We are going to make a few basic assumptions to help us all get on the same page. We won't work with a ton of technical knowledge, so don't assume that you have to spend years in college to get this done. But you do need to know your way around a computer. If you can't do a basic search online or find the settings on some of your favorite and most-visited webpages, then this is going to be a challenge.

We will also assume that you use some of the most common search engines and sites out there. We will go through quite a few of these to check the security settings and see whether there is something in them that may be holding onto your data. The bad news is that you must actively go through and make changes and tell the site to stop following you and collecting your information. The good news is that this is actually pretty easy to work with, so don't worry about it taking hours or being too technical.

A significant point to keep in mind is that the recommendations made are not the perfect solution. As with all technical solutions, they can get outdated pretty quickly, or maybe they are too restrictive, or maybe they aren't secure enough for you. But the intention behind the changes is what's important for your, and others', data privacy.

WHAT TO EXPECT

What to expect during this process will largely depend on your personal pain threshold. Some of the steps you can take will be easy, and others will seem impossible to live with. Hopefully, you'll settle on a balance that works for you.

One thing you should know is that companies will attempt to prevent you from protecting your privacy. It is in their corporate interest to keep your private data flowing into their database. That is, after all, how they make money. At some points in the process of protecting yourself, it may seem like the big companies are throwing a temper tantrum and generally being vindictive, and sometimes punitive. You may notice that they try to make it harder for you to enjoy their services when you begin to protect your own data. They may even make some services completely unavailable to you until you restore their ability to track you again. They may even seem desperate and begin making "too good to be true" offers and discounts in exchange for your personal info. One big company even bribes you with credits that can be cashed in for real money via gift cards. We'll discuss this in the next chapter.

This process won't be easy, but it will definitely be done if you take a little time to prepare, and be aware of, your online practices. Now that you've been warned, let's get into the ugly details.

1 / AVOID THE BIG BOYS

The "GAFAM" (Google, Amazon, Facebook, Apple, and Microsoft) are the five dominant internet companies that own many popular services, and often operate under a different name (e.g., WhatsApp and Instagram for Facebook).

Many of these are apps and search engines that we enjoy using, track our usage and hold onto information about us. They can use this data for a variety of reasons. For the most part, it is to make more money. Some of these companies will sell the information to advertisers to increase profits. Marketers in all industries want to learn more about their customers, such as what they will purchase, where the consumers are, and what will appeal to these individuals overall.

These major companies, who have already done a lot of work for us, and who have gained our trust, can gather up a ton of information and then sell it to the interested marketers. We assume this is not a big deal, and that the company is not giving away too much about us. But it is almost scary how much details these companies are actually digging up on us, and advertisers are eating it up.

We aren't trying to infer that you should completely avoid these companies and never have anything to do with them again. But having a bit of caution and awareness that they can *and* do take your information, without permission, and sell it to other parties—often without sharing who these other parties are—can help you to keep yourself safe online.

GOOGLE

All of us have used Google at one point or another to help us get things done. It is one of the top search engines out there, and it is the name behind YouTube, so if you spend time watching videos there, then you are familiar with Google very well. In fact, Google is so well-known that it is the de facto name in search, though there are many others, and many of its services, including Google Maps, Gmail, and some other options, are considered leaders in their categories.

We often use Google because it is free. You can use several services developed by Google, such as maps, Gmail, search engines, translate and even YouTube without having to pay anything. All of these free services sound good in theory but are going to require giving away your personal information. Google claims it does this to provide you with better ad experiences that are targeted and personalized, but they often do it without us knowing and can easily sell our information to another party at their discretion.

In 2015, Google launched a new program where your profile would be keyed back to the email address you prefer to use. This is known as Customer Match, and it is a way to ensure the advertiser's brand is right there with the right message at the times when the customer will be most receptive to seeing that information. The promise that is made here is huge, but it is meant to entice marketers to utilize the service in hopes of gaining attention from consumers who would most likely use the product or service that is being advertised.

Which brings us to the point of the type of information Google will collect in order to make this process happen. Similar with Facebook and a few of the other options we will discuss in this chapter, there is a lot of information that Google will rely on. This includes details of how you use Google's services, how you interact with some of the other websites that also rely on AdWords and other Google technologies, your credit card information, telephone number, email address, name, device details, and the search queries that you use.

And this is just the beginning of what they will collect. This information is stored in the local browser storage of your personal or work computer, and this is going to be way more than what happens with a traditional site relying on cookies. If you do not put the right security features on your account, then the information is public, and Google can use them however they want.

According to Google, anything that is public is fair game for them to use. So, if you have given your email to other users, or there is some other information that helps identify you and you have given this away, then Google is able to show this data publicly. If your Google Profile is visible, then that can be shown as well.

The good news is that Google does allow you to have some freedom to make changes and tailor what you are sharing and what they can use. But you have to go through and make those changes yourself. This is sometimes difficult and takes some time, and with Google changing their policies on a consistent basis, usually as a way to benefit themselves, you will need to go through and check these security settings regularly too.

AMAZON

We also have to take some time to look at Amazon and all the factors that we need to be aware of with this company. Most of us are familiar with Amazon and often use their products and services. We may like to get our Christmas shopping done on their online site because it is simple and easy, and there is a plethora of customer reviews to help determine the value of an item. We may use a Kindle to read or have an Alexa device at home to assist with requests, like playing music, placing orders or asking questions.

Due to the wide variety of products and services that Amazon can offer to those who shop with them, they also have access to a diverse and vast amount of information regarding their customers. In addition to some of the specifics that we expect, like our names and our payment and order histories when we are done shopping, they will also have an abundance of information that is personal, which they could sell to some of their third-party companies to make more money. In some cases, many believe Alexa is getting a hold of some of our personal conversations and that can be extremely dangerous as well.

It is estimated right now that Amazon could make up to $1 billion solely on advertising revenue in the near future. This may not put it at the top compared to some of the other sites out there, but considering that the main goal of Amazon is to sell more products, and not to sell more advertising, this is an alarming number that we need to spend some time on.

And Amazon is nowhere near done with this. So far, Amazon has been good about keeping a lot of its advertising ambitions to itself, that is until 2012. That was when Amazon's Vice President of Global Sales, Lisa Utzschneider, attended Advertising Week in New York and showed all of the different ways that Amazon could provide for advertising clients to their ideal customers. From ad-targeting data to clicks and more, whether it happened on their website or on one of their devices, Amazon opened up a whole new world for marketers to really enjoy.

What ultimately helps to put Amazon over the top is the vast amount of information that they have on their customers. If you use any of the products from Amazon, they can hold onto that and learn more about you. Considering people throughout the world have these products, and many have more than one, it is no wonder Amazon has extensive amounts of data that can help their marketers specifically target the right demographics to make the most money as well.

Another appealing process to marketers is that Amazon is further down the sales funnel than Google or Bing or some of the other options. Amazon has actual information about what their customers have purchased in the past and what they are more likely to purchase in the future. They don't just gather information on what people have searched for and clicked on. They can take it a bit further and list out what the customer actually bought on their site. This is a goldmine for a lot of marketers who want to really target their ads and create content that can bring more profits.

If you are a fan of some of the features and products that come with Amazon, then you must be careful about what you do and say around some of them. For example, how safe do you think your information is around the popular voice-controlled Alexa products from Amazon? Recently, Amazon has come under fire for how Alexa gathers and uses names. And this could be a big problem considering how many people around the world have purchased products with Alexa in them. It is believed that the little microphones inside these devices, the ones that hear you and answer your questions or complete other requests for you, could be used to listen in on you, even when you are not using the product.

For many users, this seems like a crazy idea reserved for conspiracy theorists and no one else. However, according to Bloomberg, Amazon now has a network throughout the world that has thousands of these little eavesdroppers listening secretly to the audio that was secretly recorded through Echo devices. Amazon claims that they are simply listening and collecting audio files only when you talk to ensure that Alexa can understand the speech patterns of humans and react better when you use the product.

Even though Amazon claims that these devices are not able to hear what happens in your home unless the word "Alexa" is said first—and they state that no one is actually eavesdropping—there have been several cases to show this is not true. For example, there was a case in which two Amazon employees overheard what sounded like a sexual assault case when listening to the devices. Amazon has since stated they have more procedures in place to follow when there are serious situations overheard on the device, but this also tells us that someone, somewhere, is hearing our private conversations when we use these devices, and this is never a good thing for us.

Using these devices may seem like a great idea. But if you are not using them in the right way, and you don't make sure they are turned off, then it is possible for someone else to overhear your private conversations and things that happen in the privacy of your own home. And is there any proof that those who hear it won't try to use it for their own advantages?

FACEBOOK

There have been a lot of controversies that involve using Facebook, and it seems like each day we can find more and more of these that should make us wary about sharing any information with this company. A common theme here, though, is that Facebook appears to be a machine that is always hungry for data and that their biggest goal overall is to get more data from their users and then classify them as accurately as possible. They can then sell that information and make more money.

This alone should make us worried about using this service at all. And if you do use it, you need to be cautious with the way you work with it. Facebook, as they have proven time and time again, is more interested in learning how to make money from you than your actual safety and security online. Let's look at a few examples of how this works.

Most of us know by now that Facebook can track our location. Sometimes we encourage this by adding a location to some of our pictures to let others know where we are. But while we realize this is an optional feature, we may not fully realize all of the things that Facebook can do with this information, or even how many ways this company is able to track us.

There are five different ways that Facebook is able to track your location. And if you are online on your phone or another device that you carry around with you, it is likely you are logged in and someone else could figure out where you are at any time. Here are the five main ways Facebook can use their tracking service to collect more data on you:

1. **Using location data:** This is actually one of the easiest methods for the company to know where you are.

They can figure out your current location, the history of places you have been, and even the Nearby Friends option. Even if you take the time to turn these off, Facebook can still track you and give you relevant ads using your Wi-Fi and your IP address. According to security researchers, unfortunately there aren't any combinations that you can use in your settings to prevent you from being tracked in this way.

2. **Tracking the movement of your mouse:** Earlier in 2018, Facebook admitted they could collect your information from TV, phones, computers and any other devices that are connected to them, including your mouse movements, to collect data and provide you with personalized content. This sounds great for you because it is personalized, but really, it means that the company is selling information on your device IDs, file types and names, operating system, hardware and more.

3. **Using the connected app:** If you have some apps on your phone, then Facebook is able to gather that information as well. Even if you are using a dating app or a delivery app to make life more convenient, Facebook has tools that allow them to extract this information too.

4. **By the apps that some of your friends install:** Even some of the apps that your friends will install through Facebook can gather information on them, as well as you. The best way to deal with this one is to go to the apps setting on Facebook. Click and remove the ones that you do not want to use or are not comfortable with.

5. **Looking at your online movements.** This one has Facebook working on many things at once. Not only can they track the window you are in to see whether it is

in the foreground or the background, but they can also see what items you are purchasing.

This is a lot of information for Facebook to collect. And most of it comes from sources that have nothing to do with Facebook in the first place. This should put you on alert that something is wrong here and you will need to guard your information as carefully as possible.

Facebook has gotten into quite a bit of trouble recently for the type and the amount of data they have sold to other companies, especially to their marketers. This social media site has access to a ton of data and they can use and sell it any way they want. However, Facebook still denies this practice. They state that they have never provided others access to personal data without the necessary permission. They go on to talk about how they have not seen any evidence of data being misused.

While they do maintain that they are innocent and not negatively using the data, Facebook does acknowledge they should have taken the right steps to prevent any third parties from being able to tap into the data of the users, and they have gone through and stopped this practice to protect the privacy of their users.

Many do not believe that Facebook has taken the right steps to protect those who use their site, stating that some third-party companies and products have been able to retrieve private messages of some users, see personal information, and more. Whether Facebook is allowing this to happen and selling the information to make more profits, or they are doing what they can to protect the information, there is definitely a loophole here that allows third parties to gather your information without your permission. It's in your best interest to learn ways to protect your information so no one can get it if you don't want them to.

APPLE

Even Apple will spend time tracking what their users are doing online. This is such a profitable strategy for companies that we should start assuming most of the other services we use will do this. And it's automatic unless we go through and purposely turn this feature off. So, given the opportunity to increase market share, it makes sense Apple will also collect data.

Think about all the products and services available from Apple. And then think about how many people use these on a regular basis. Think about how many of these products you use. And if the product can get online at all, you can bet that Apple will gather your information and use it for their own needs.

Since these companies don't have to be open about this collection of information, it's hard to know whether they are using it in a way that we can trust. And since Apple has so many products that we can use, it brings in the potential for Apple to gather an extraordinary amount of information on us.

A recent lawsuit done in May of 2019 reveals how bad this problem has gotten. The lawsuit states that Apple has been selling data based on the listening habits of its users out of the iTunes store, along with numerous other information about the customers, which is all done without consumer consent.

According to this lawsuit, the data of the users is sold for about $136 per 1,000 users. To make it worse, the buyers of this data are then able to customize and add other personal information to their liking, including marital status, household income, age, and gender and then resell this data to another third party in the process. By this time, we are only a few companies removed from Apple, and your data is floating around for the highest bidder to grab and use how they want.

MICROSOFT

Even Microsoft has decided to join the game and start their own search engine. Why wouldn't they? Data collection is a big moneymaker and since Google and others have used it, why wouldn't one of the bigger names in software and technology? Microsoft came to the game kind of late, though. While Google, Yahoo and some other search engines have been around for a long time, and are the standards of the online searching world, Microsoft's search engine, called Bing, is a collaboration between Microsoft and Yahoo and is relatively new.

Despite being so new, Bing is already considered one of the main players in the market. They have many subscribers and many more searches done on a regular basis. What is their secret? How are they getting all of these searchers, especially since the product they offer is very similar to what is already on the market through Google and other similar sites?

One differentiating aspect is that Bing uses bribery, of sorts, to bring in the searchers. While Bing garnered some attention and brought many people over to it right from the start, it wasn't enough for Microsoft. So, to solve this problem, they decided to work with a strategy that has not been seen much since the early internet days of the late '90s and early 00s, and they provide rewards to their loyal customers who use the service regularly.

There are actually a number of methods that users can rely on in order to get rewards. The easiest way to do this is to earn points based on your searches. As long as you are logged into your account when you search, you can receive points, up to a certain amount, for those searches. You can then redeem these for Amazon gift cards, Xbox Live and more.

You can also sign up and install what is known as the Bing bar, which is compatible with IE (Internet Explorer) from Microsoft, and you will get 250 points. One hundred points in Bing will convert into 100 points in Microsoft, which is basically about $1.25.

Beyond the 250 points that you will get right out of the gate, you can conduct more searches online to get more points. Each search will provide you with more points, which you can save to accrue enough to use toward video games, Bing merchandise, random things, and even some gift cards to popular stores. There are limits on how many searches you can do each day to earn points, but it is still a pretty good deal for those who will go online to search anyway.

When you sign into your account, which is a requirement to get the points, Bing is able to track your movements. They can then sell this information to others for advertising and other reasons without you knowing where that information is going. And their method is working. Many people use Bing to get the points because it is simple, and Microsoft is able to make a ton of money out of it. The important question here though, is whether your data is being used well or if this is harming your security?

WE ALL LIKE TO USE SOCIAL MEDIA. IT'S A GREAT WAY IN OUR modern world to keep up with those we are close to and to ensure we are really able to communicate and see what everyone is up to. Many of us will admit that we spend way too much time on social media, but the main idea of its origin and purpose has been beneficial for most of us.

As we talked about a bit in our previous discussion about Facebook and some of the other common options for social media and being online, we need to be careful about the amount of information we are sharing online. Facebook and other similar sites are able to take that data and use it in any manner that they would like, usually in order to make money. The good news is that there are some simple methods we can use to make sure we keep our information safe and to make it harder for these companies to profit off personal details that should not be released, at least not without our permission.

FACEBOOK

The first site that we need to look at is Facebook. This company alone has brought about a lot of negative media attention when it comes to the amount of data they collect and how it is used. From taking information and selling it to marketers to hiding certain political ads that don't meet with their agenda, Facebook seems to be in hot water quite a bit of the time.

Because of this, and the fact Facebook has made it known that profits are their primary motivating factor rather than their user's interests, it's a good idea to learn some of the ways you can keep that data safe and make sure Facebook is not able to use it the way that they want. These ideas include:

Turn Off the Tracking

In the previous chapter, we reviewed five different ways that Facebook is able to track your location. Sometimes, they can even track what websites you were on, and other search history and this has nothing to do with Facebook. How many times have you gotten off Facebook, then browsed your favorite store, or looked up a product or service on your preferred search engine? Then when you go back to Facebook later, there are ads all over the place for that same product or service. It doesn't seem to matter if you purchased that item or not.

The reason you're seeing those familiar links or images on your feed is because Facebook can track what you are doing online—which is definitely not something that most of us are comfortable with. It is one thing to have a social media site keep track of the apps and the movements we use when we are actually on their site, but when they start tracking what we do off of it, then we can all agree their tactics are a bit out of hand.

Fortunately, there are a few methods that we can use to keep Facebook from tracking our locations.

If you are using an Android App:

1. Go to Settings.
2. Go to your Apps.
3. Click on Facebook.
4. While you are there, you can click on the Mobile data and Wi-Fi.
5. Turn off the Background data.
6. Configure Facebook.

If you are using an iPhone or iPad:

1. Launch into the Settings App on your device.
2. Tap on Privacy.
3. Tap on the Location Services.
4. Tap on Facebook.
5. Tap on Never.

Control Permissions

We can also prevent Facebook from having permission to save our location history at all. Maybe you like to take the time to use the Friends Nearby and the check-in feature that Facebook has to offer, and in exchange, you don't mind sharing some of the data on your location to get those. You can certainly leave this tracking on, but just make sure to set it so that it will only be able to track when you are using the app, and then you can turn off the part that saves your history. To do this, use the following steps:

1. Open the app for Facebook on your device.

2. Tap on the More tab. You should see this near the bottom right of your screen.
3. Scroll down and tap on the Settings.
4. Click to open the Account Settings and then on Location.
5. Turn the switch for having Location History Off.

Delete History

If Facebook has already had time to track some of your location histories in the past, we can also turn this off and delete that history from your device. This can help keep you protected and keep others out of your information. To do this, you can use the following steps:

1. Open up the Facebook app as we did before.
2. Tap on the tab for More found on the right part of your screen on the bottom.
3. Scroll down a bit until you see the Settings tab. Click on that.
4. Click on Activity Log and then filter.
5. Click on the Location History before clearing it.
6. Tap to confirm.

These steps will help to delete all of your stored location histories. Even if you plan to use these apps on occasion, it is a good idea to erase the history and do the purge on occasion. That will make sure that no one is able to figure out where you have been months ago.

Another thing to note is that we will need to go through and do the same steps to get Instagram taken care of. This is a company owned by Facebook, but they will still gather up all of the information they can about their customers, whether you are on Facebook, Instagram, or both. You will need to go into your settings on Instagram as well and do the same thing to make sure that the company is not able to steal your information and keep track of you.

TWITTER

There are several issues that can come up when using Twitter for some of your social media needs. This one, just like all of the others, has no problem with taking some of your information, and more of it than we may realize at first, then selling it to other people to make a profit. This is never a good thing, and since so much of our personal information is sold for profit simply because we use the sites, we need to be extra careful.

However, there is a third-party advertising company that Twitter owns, known as MoPub, which is in a lot of trouble right now. In January of 2020, Grindr, a social network and dating app, got into some problems because of the way it collected and shared data. They were using MoPub advertising during the time that they got into trouble, which helped to bring to light some of the methods that Twitter has been using and promoting.

While it can be agreed on that Grindr was not in the clear, they took the time to build up a platform that would encourage users to be very open with personal information that was considered potentially dangerous and sensitive, and in turn, they pretty much invited other advertisers to take as much of that personal data as they would like. In the meantime, Twitter has suspended Grindr and has made them look like an anomaly and one bad actor who used the advertising wrong.

There are many though who believe that Twitter is being hypocritical. This is because, though Grindr got caught doing things they shouldn't, they were pretty much using the ad tool from Twitter exactly how it was designed to be used. MoPub is an ad tool that is able to collect lots of personal data and then shares that to help modern marketers do their job. To really get a good understanding of how this ecosystem is supposed to work, and where this ad tool and Grindr can fit in, we need to look at something known as RTB or real-time binding.

RTB is an automatic process that will share data like crazy whenever there is a third-party app on your device. First, a company, such as Grindr, will decide to utilize that app and monetize it. To do this, they would work with the Supply-Side Platform (or SSP), which is what MoPub is all about. The SSP will basically be a company that website publishers and app developers will hire to make sure they can sell all of their space with advertising. When you install the app for Grindr on your phone or somewhere else, you will also get a big piece of code from MoPub. After doing a bit of configuration at the beginning, Grindr is going to leave some of the details that are needed for serving ads and data sharing to MoPub.

What's amazing is the process that's used here. When someone decides to open up the Grindr app, MoPub's code will be there, ready to work its magic. The process that happens here include:

- The code can gather up as much data out of the user's phone as possible. This is then sent over to MoPub.
- Then MoPub is able to link the data that it gets from Grindr with what it can gather up from other sources. This includes all of the other apps that work with MoPub, including sites like the Weather Channel.
- Then this is packaged up into a bid request and will include a lot of your information like interest keywords, age, gender, location and more.

- MoPub will then work to send in a bid request to hundreds of demand-side platforms or DSPs. These are the companies that advertisers work with in order to target and send out the advertisements of their choosing.
- Each of the DSPs that get this request can then link the device ID over to the user's profile and get more information.
- Then the DSP can submit a bid to serve an ad to that user, and they can even choose the time when they want to do this.
- MoPub will then determine the bidder who wins and will have an auction that will let everyone else know.
- The advertiser who wins will see its ad go to the phone of the user. This will also allow the advertiser to come in and get more information that they need, right from the device itself.

While Grindr may not have been doing things the way they should, they were using an app that made things worse. Twitter is trying to defend all that this app can do, and they talk about how it can be useful for a personalized experience. But it is designed to get into apps and phones and take personal information, which can lead to a serious loss in privacy.

REDDIT

Now that we have taken a bit of time to talk about some of the bad guys who are out there in the world of advertising, it is time to switch gears a bit and look at Reddit. This is a popular site with many people using it each day. But it is also the one that is the most privacy-conscious out of all of them. They do not sell all your information to the highest bidder; in fact, they don't really collect that much information to start with.

When you sign up for a Reddit account, you only need to provide a few details. You can sign up with a simple username and password. They will not ask your name, your age, or for any other information from you. Once you pick the username or password, then you can jump right in and enjoy some of the features, though they are more limited than a few other options you may find out there. They don't even require an email address! However, the drawback of not using an email address is you that cannot request a password reset if you forget your password.

One thing that you will notice between Reddit and some of the others is the lack of features and benefits. The other sites will use ways to entice by giving away apps that you want to use, gift cards to keep you coming back to use them, and more. That is why most of us agree to have only some data taken. We usually assume that they only take a little bit of data, but as we have already seen in this book, they actually take quite a bit.

Reddit is a little bit different here. They do not take and sell your data. But they also do not offer a lot of cool apps and features for us to enjoy. They are easy to use, and you are sure to find some useful attributes. But it is a basic website with a simple search for it. There aren't features to track you or features to keep you coming back. Figuring out a good balance between keeping your data safe, like what Reddit can do, and getting some cool features from Facebook and Instagram, is the big challenge here.

OPTIONS TO STAY SAFE ON SOCIAL MEDIA

The best option to keep you safe online is to avoid social media altogether. There is so much information that these companies can get their hands on. And because they can make a huge profit from it, they are more than willing to track you and take as much information and data as they can—and they don't even ask permission ahead of time.

In our modern world, it is hard to give up social media entirely. If you can, that is one of the best ways to keep your data safe. If not, that's fine. Think of the social media sites and apps that you just can't give up, perhaps the top two or three. Then get rid of the others. The sites that are on your phone or device, the ones that you barely, if ever, use, can still collect data and will put you at risk. Keep your choices to the ones that you plan to use on a regular basis and remove all the rest.

There are also social media apps that are more data-privacy conscious than the big players like Facebook, Instagram and Twitter, and function almost identically. However, with less popularity, there are drastically less users to interact with.

If you must use social media, or you just can't give up one of the platforms, then the next best option is accessing it through your web browser instead. This gives you some added security because you can utilize your ad blockers and other privacy tools. Plus, if your computer just stays at your home and never goes anywhere with you, then it won't be able to track you, so consider using the social media site through there. Never, ever access the social media site through their native application because this lets them in and allows them to take all of your data with ease. If you're on your smartphone, you can even add the webpage bookmark to your home screen and mimic an app's appearance.

And finally, when you do use an app or download a new one, make sure that you take the time to go to your settings and change as much of it as you can to protect your privacy. Turn off the tracking and anything else that will allow the app to retrieve and sell your information to anyone they would like.

We took some time to talk about some of the different options that we can choose from when it comes to social media, and how many of these sites can take our data and use it to make a lot of money. With that understanding, it's time to take a look at some of the different hardware options that you can consider to make sure you are keeping unwanted people out, and your data inside and safe. Let's take a look at some of the computers, phones, thermostats, smart TVs and more that you can choose to keep your data safe.

THE SNOWDEN LAPTOP

We'll begin by taking a look at a few laptop choices you can go with if you want to make sure your data is safe, and no one will be able to get into it in the first place. You can certainly make your own personal computer safer, but these are designed to make sure no one can access your information and can keep you safer than other options.

Purism is a company that creates these kinds of computers. They are sometimes called the Snowden Laptop because they are really good at keeping your information private and will respect any digital life you have at the time. There are a number of reasons to go with this kind of computer, especially if you are worried about keeping people out of your system.

When you spend time on social media, store files on a cloud, search online, or chat and message on an app, it is likely that you are being tracked. This is all done by a market that will use your phone or your laptop to get as much information from you as possible. As discussed before, this information can then be sold between many companies, and you don't get any say in whether this happens or not. With Purism and one of their computers, you can have the choice to not give away this data to companies who only use it for profit.

These computers have been designed in every aspect to respect your own digital life. They all come with physical hardware kill switches for the microphone and camera and then all of the back-doors that are commonly used for hardware will be disabled. This allows you to turn everything off and use the computer how you want, without the marketers and other apps coming in and stealing your information.

Basically, this is going to keep the marketers out. Unless you personally send the information out and give it to them, they will not be able to find backdoors and other methods to gather that information. This is bad news for those companies who want the data to make more money, but it is really good news for you.

KEEPING YOUR PHONE SAFE

Since so many of us rely on our phones to send emails, look online, and browse social media, it is important that we use some caution when it comes to picking out the right phones for our needs as well.

There are a few options that we can use in order to pick out the right phones. The first one is known as Cipher. This comes with a shutter that provides us with privacy on our camera, a kill switch for the microphone, a switch to wipe the device, a touch contact exchange, and protection on the boot loader, which is a series of commands and software that run upon startup.

Cipher is also able to provide us with some security for the software on it. This is crucial to make sure that we are not going to be taken advantage of through the apps and software we rely on. Some of the important security options on the software we can use include:

- The ability to switch between the ciphOS and Android. ciphOS is a cipher Linux operating system that is designed to be as secure as possible.
- Single-use key encryption.
- Switches automatically between the IP and VPN every 30 seconds so it is hard to catch where you are.
- None of your conversations or the data in them is written to a disk.
- There isn't a central messaging server, so your data stays safe.

Another option to use is KATIM, which is considered as one of the most secure smartphones out there. It is based on a version of Android for the operating system, but it is going to work a bit differently than some of the other phones you may use. For example, when you boot up KATIM, it will check the software and if it detects some modifications, the phone will not turn on. It then continues to monitor the integrity of the environment frequently while making sure that your phone will be safe all the time, even from some common security threats.

When picking out a phone, consider the carrier as well. These companies can sometimes be part of the problem too. We need to consider how they protect our privacy and read the fine print to find out whether our data is used or sold by the company. If your phone carrier does use and sell the data, then it may be time to switch.

PICKING A ROUTER

A router is a device for networking that will forward packets of data between different computer networks. Routers are specific for performing functions of directing the traffic over the internet as well. Data that we are able to send through the internet, including email and web pages, will be in the form of data packets.

We want to make sure that we have a router with some good security features. Many times the routers we receive from our wireless carriers can be good, but since we hold onto them for a long time, it is possible that they will get outdated and not work as well as we intended them to. There are a few options to help us get started.

Anonabox Router

If you want security without having to build one yourself, then Anonabox is a good solution. This provides you with a lot of the features that you want, makes it easy to search the internet, and provides you with all the security features you need. Some of the ways that we can use Anonabox include:

- It makes it easier to get to the dark web without being found.
- You can use it with Tor (a privacy-oriented browser).
- It helps to deter companies from collecting your data.
- It can stop ads that are used for remarketing.
- Extends out your range on the Wi-Fi if needed.
- It can help you to be online anonymously.
- Keeps your location secret and provides you with online browsing privacy so you can get things done.
- Keeps the hackers out at the same time.

Building Your Own Router

It is even possible to build up your own router, though this may require some technical knowledge before you start. This allows you to add in the exact hardware and software that you want and can ensure that your router is as safe as we can get. It may lack a bit of the other features that you see with other routers, so we need to be careful when picking one of these out. But it is also a good way to keep yourself secure.

There are a few options and instructions that you can follow when it is time to build up your own router system. You can look for one that suits your needs the best and will offer you the right balance of security and features that you are looking for.

OTHER DANGERS TO BE CAREFUL WITH

While we are here, we need to take some time to show caution with the software and hardware that we frequently use. There are many great tools and devices that we can use regularly, which can make our lives better. But we have to consider whether these are safe to use, and how much data they are taking from us when we use them.

For example, Google Home and Alexa are both virtual assistant devices. Depending on how connected we are, we may use them to order groceries for us, ask questions, request food delivery, turn lights on and off, change the temperature, and much more. If there is an app associated with an action, these two options can help to get them done.

However, if you have a connected home like this, it is going to set you up for handing over a lot of information to Google and Amazon. They can learn about your home, what questions you ask, what temperature your home is set at and at which times (hence, revealing to them when you are most likely home or not), and more. And there are concerns that these microphones are able to catch on to some of the personal conversations we have as well, which can make these voice-controlled systems that much more dangerous to work with.

Another popular device that is being used right now is known as the Ring doorbell. This is an app that works with Android and is known to be great for harvesting plenty of data according to one investigation done by EFF or (Electronic Frontier Foundation). There are even claims that say Ring will deliver updates on usage over to Facebook, even if that user doesn't have a Facebook account. While it may be a great idea for you to monitor what's going on around your home, it can also be used against you.

EFF tested this out by doing a dynamic analysis on the Ring device mobile app. This was done with the multiproxy tool going through the access point for Wi-Fi that was connected to the doorbell. Through that, the proxy tool was able to analyze and intercept the flows of HTTPS to and from the device. And the information that was collected included lots of PII, or personally identifiable information, data on the device and carrier of the user, and unique identifiers, so companies could track when you went on other apps, and even information on your home network.

This means that while you may be using the device to see who is coming to your doorstep, and maybe even as a way to keep your home secure, it is possible that the Ring company, or Amazon, is able to take a lot of information from you and use it for their advantages as well.

What about that smart thermostat you've added to your home? This is an efficient way to automate your home's temperature based on the time of day and other features. So, if you have it off to conserve energy during the day, then you can set it to start warming up shortly before you return, allowing you to have a nice heated home when you get there.

While the Nest device is not something that could be accessed from a remote location, that doesn't mean that you are safe. In fact, many people choose to purchase the Nest device from somewhere outside of the original manufacturer, meaning they can get it for a good deal on Craigslist or eBay. It may be safe originally, but if someone purchases a bunch of these, they could possibly load spyware onto them before sending them off to you. You would not suspect anything because the tool would work well. But someone else could use it to watch you, take your information, and more.

It is even possible that someone could take over your whole network from the Nest if they want. Whether they use this to collect data from you or to attempt a hack, it is still going to make a difference. Since the Nest will sit on the network just like your computer, it could easily be set up to spoof a type of data packet, called ARP packets, to act as the router and identify all the devices on your network. This is an effective way for the hacker to capture all of the network traffic of the target computer, and then all your information is open for the hacker to enjoy.

MODEM

Picking out a good modem is very important. The right one is going to make a big difference in how reliable your connection to the internet is, and how safe your information is when it's transmitted back and forth. It is often best to use your own modem instead of the modem offered by your internet service provider (ISP). This can save you upwards of $168 a year alone. And because so many people are cutting the cable to work with some of the streaming services, it is likely the costs will go up as these companies try to offset some of their expenses. How long do you think it will be before these companies try to get your data and sell it to keep their shrinking profit margins?

You do not have to spend time making your own modem unless you want to. Instead, there are a number of options out there you can choose. And these will help you to stay protected. And since they have a one-time cost, which usually isn't that high, you can save money while protecting your information.

RASPBERRY PI

If you don't mind doing a bit of the work on your own, then working with the Raspberry Pi option is a great choice to make. First, let's look at what Raspberry Pi is all about. These are a series of small computers with just one board. They were originally designed to help teach computer science to students, so you won't have to worry about these being too difficult to understand or hard to work with. They are often used in robotics and for some single projects, but we can design this to work with our own personal computers and some larger projects as well.

There are also a few great DIY projects for the Raspberry Pi family that can keep your system safe. One of these is known as

Pi-hole. This allows you to work with your favorite operating system and then will block all of the advertisements and the data mining that tries to come into your computer. It is considered the black hole for advertising on the internet, in that it refuses to let those bots and codes come in, ensuring that you can keep your information safe and secure the whole time. It is simple software to add to your Raspberry Pi computer, especially if you are already using the Raspbian operating system, and can help to prevent marketers from getting your information.

NEXTCLOUD

Many of us are familiar with the idea of the Cloud. There are many options available for the Cloud, and we can select the one that is the best for our needs. The point of using these is to make sure your valuable pictures, files and more are always safe and accessible, even if something happens to your computer.

The idea behind it is great, but not all of these areas are as safe and secure as they promised. Many of them, including the Google Cloud, have had trouble with keeping hackers out. And since these companies are known for collecting data and using it to make money, it is likely that some of your data is vulnerable if you continue to use these clouds.

This doesn't mean that you are out of luck and can't use these at all. But it does mean that you will need to pick a good one. And that is where NextCloud can come in. This is known as a type of software that is used to create and then use file hosting services. It is similar in functionality to what we see in Dropbox, but it doesn't offer any off-premise hosting for your file storage. It is free and open-sourced, which means that you can install it anytime and anywhere you would like. You can even use it on your own devices. It has a lot more security and safety features.

Whether you use NextCloud or not, it is best to go with a cloud service that has a proven record of being secure. Do your research before going with one over another to make sure your files will be safe. You don't want to risk having your personal files and other information being used in a way that you don't agree with.

4 / SOFTWARE TO CONSIDER

In addition to some of the hardware that we talked about before, we also need to spend some time looking at a few software options. Often it is the software that can cause the biggest issues to your safety. If the software is not made the best, and there are backdoors and other issues with it, then marketers and other companies are more than willing to exploit some of these and take any information they want. Let's dive in and take a look at some of the software we can use, the ones that are the best, and which ones we should avoid.

CHOOSING YOUR OPERATING SYSTEM

The first line of defense we need to consider is our operating system and how we can utilize this for our needs. This is what will run all of the other applications and software we need on our computer. Some are safer than the others, and whatever you decide will make a big difference in how well things work.

WINDOWS

Windows is a very common operating system that is used throughout the world. Microsoft has made a name for itself and many computers have been purchased by customers with this operating system already installed on it. This great marketing technique allows the consumer to be familiar with this operating system. And since a majority of us are not familiar with using operating systems or how to download another one, we just keep it there, even if Windows is the best option for us to use.

While Windows is popular, the security that comes with it is going to depend on the size of the user base that has it installed. Windows is going to provide us a massive playing field for malware and other viruses. Because it is such a vast operating system and used by so many people, hackers like to go after this. It may be hard to get on, but if they can manage, they have a ton of potential for sending adware, malware, and other issues. Even with the beefed-up security that Microsoft is trying to set up, this is still a goldmine and many hackers will continue to go after it.

MAC OS

So, if the operating system that is the most popular is considered one of the biggest targets, then it would make sense to go with another option for security, right? This falls on the idea that we can have security through obscurity, which can be a bad idea because you are giving into complacency and that can allow hackers to get in.

While Mac OS is considered a safer alternative to working with Windows, it is not perfect. And there are still a lot of attackers who are happy to try to break through this system. It is more secure compared to Windows, and it has a great track record when it comes to keeping people out. But it is still not the best option if you can choose from all the operating systems.

LINUX

The winner of this game is Linux. There are not that many choices when it comes to which computers use this system, but it is still able to offer a lot of protection that Windows or Mac OS cannot. The biggest factor with Linux is that often the user has to know how to do tasks from the command line, which is a bit different than what we're used to doing with the other operating systems. But once you get familiar with using the command line, instead of the graphics to move around, you will find that Linux is one of the most secure options out there.

The learning curve on using this system is one of the main reasons that a lot of people do not choose to work with Linux. The command line requires some knowledge with coding to make it work. But it is safe and secure, and it is easy to download on any computer without costs, so that is an added benefit to using this system.

The good news is that modern distributions of Linux include a graphical desktop environment, like Windows. These new versions feel much more familiar and are easier to work with. Also, much of the same software you're already using is available for Linux.

MOBILE OPERATING SYSTEMS

It is becoming more common and prevalent that we are moving our lives off the desktop computers and over to a mobile device. And similar to the computer, these mobile phones need to have an operating system to help them run. There are a few options that you are able to use to help run your smartphone, and we need to take a look at the positive and the negative of each one.

ANDROID

The first mobile operating system that we will take a look at is known as Android. This one is kind of unique in that it is a modified version of Linux, and it was designed to work with mobile devices that have a touchscreen, including tablets and smartphones. This operating system was developed by its own company, Android Inc, but then in 2005, it was bought by Google. We already know what Google is able and willing to do with the data it collects from customers, so this is something we should already be a bit worried about if choosing this operating system. This can be seen in a few other options as well, including iOS.

In 2013, there was a disclosure that revealed many intelligence agencies in America and a few other companies were able to gather up the data found in Android and iPhone devices. This allowed them to get a hold of all sorts of information about the phones, including the notes, location, emails and more. This happened on more than one operating system, but it still should put us on the lookout because we never know who is able to gather up our information.

This is also one of the most common operating systems that are used on tablets and smartphones, which means that it is the one you are most likely to use. It is also more likely that this one is going to be more susceptible to attacks and hacks from others, so it is important to use precautions when using this system.

IOS

If you are a fan of Apple products, including their phones, then you will be familiar with iOS. This is a mobile operating system that Apple created and is used only for their products. It is going to be the operating system in charge of running the phones and other mobile devices sold by Apple. It is very unlikely that you will see this operating system on a product that does not come from Apple.

There are a few options you can enjoy when it comes to the safety and security that iOS will provide to your phone. It has a Face ID or scanner that can make it easier to unlock the device, to log into some of your chosen applications, and even to make purchases. There is also a secure boot, a passcode, a touch ID, and more to make sure that your information stays safe.

Just like we saw with some of the options with computers, iOS is a safer alternative because of the numbers compared to Android. And it is only found on Apple products. But due to the fact that a lot of people like to work with these devices, it is still vulnerable to some attacks.

LINUX

Just like Linux is a safe and easy alternative for your computer, there are also some alternatives you can install on your phones to get the same security. There are a number of these that work really well so it depends on your personal preference. Be aware from the start that these do function a little bit differently than you see with the other two aforementioned options so you may have to make some adjustments. But when it comes to the security of your phone, these can help to patch up the holes that other operating systems leave behind and can give you the best option for your time.

There are actually a few options in the Linux operating system that you can go with. What you decide on can depend on your type of phone, what you want to be able to accomplish on the phone, and what security features are the most important to you. Some of the options you can choose with Linux include Firefox, Ubuntu, Samsung Tizen, Jolla Sailfish, and Amazon Fire to name a few.

THE SECURITY SOFTWARE YOU NEED

If you want to make sure no one is able to get onto your computer and steal some of the important information on there, then you need to make sure you are using the right software to protect your entire computer. This will ensure that the hackers, and even sites like Facebook and more, are unable to access and put a lot of unnecessary information and add-ons, etc. to your system. Some of the security software systems that you can consider include:

MALWARE PROTECTION

While many of us think about putting up a good antivirus to keep our systems safe, it is sometimes easy to forget that we need to work with malware protection as well. There are a lot of reasons why this malware protection is so important and going without it can cause some issues on our computer.

First, malware protection is a good way to make sure our computer does not start slowing down. Anyone who has been infected with malware will talk about how it has made their operating system and their internet speed a lot slower. Using applications can also be kind of burdensome here because it is going to slow down with these attacks as well. Having some good malware protection in place can make a difference.

This malware protection can also help to prevent some of those popup messages on the computer. This is an annoying issue that lets us know for certain that our computer has been affected by malware. And ignoring them is just going to make it worse. Malware software can help to prevent these and will keep your whole computer safe.

And finally, the malware system functions to protect your personal information. If you do not have this protection, then hackers and others can dive in and take all of the information and data that they would like from your computer, which is exactly what we are trying to prevent.

VIRUS DETECTOR

If you want to keep your information safe, then you need to make sure you have a virus detector on your computer. This will keep a lot of the marketers and bad actors off your computer and can make sure there are no backdoors left open for a hacker to gain entry. This antivirus is going to be an essential part of your system to be secure as possible. And the best news is that you do not have to pay an arm and a leg to get good protection either. There are actually a number of options that are free to use, so you really have no excuse not to put one on your system. Some of the options include:

- AVG Free
- McAfee Antivirus Plus
- ESET NOD32 Antivirus
- Kaspersky
- Bitdefender Antivirus Plus

- Webroot SecureAnywhere
- Symantec Norton

The option that you go with can be up to personal preference and what seems the best for your needs. Just make sure you get a good antivirus that will work well and can provide you with some of the protection you need.

VPN

A VPN stands for a Virtual Private Network. It is important because it allows you an easy way to create a secure connection to some other network of your choice over the internet. You can use these to prevent others from seeing what you are doing online, or even to get on websites that are restricted based on your region.

Today, there is a lot of demand for these, though not for the original intended purpose. They were originally designed so that businesses would be able to connect to other networks securely and sometimes so that someone would be able to make a connection back to their organization network if they were at home.

These work in that they will take all of the network traffic you have and forward it over to the network. This is the point where all of the benefits, like being able to access the resources of the local network remotely and bypassing some of the censorship online, will come from. The neat thing is that most of the operating systems you work with will come with this integrated VPN support.

There are several reasons why you would want to use this VPN, and it is often best to find a reliable source and place to get this VPN outside of your own operating system. This basically allows you to go through and be invisible when you are online. No one can see where you are, where you have been and where you are going. When no one has any idea where you are online, it is impossible to gather up data on you. This may be one of the safest and most effective ways for you to move around online without encountering many issues.

Here are some great VPN options that you should consider:

1. Proton VPN
2. NordVPN
3. Mullvad VPN
4. IPVN

PASSWORD MANAGERS

The final point that we need to take a look at in this section is password managers. The password manager is simply going to be an application that you can use to store and manage the passwords you use on a wide number of online accounts. It often has some great security features to make sure you can use the passwords in the right spots without someone being able to get a hold of them.

The password manager is then able to store the password after encrypting, which helps you gain access to a specific site any time you would like, but no one else can. If you have a lot of websites that you visit on a regular basis (which is not recommended if you want to keep your information safe), then you need to use one of these password managers to make sure that your data is safe and secure all the time. You won't have to remember the passwords, and no one will be able to gain access to your passwords because the information has been encrypted.

Another bonus to using a password manager is that you can manage a different password for each site you visit. And you should. It is not recommended to use the same password at multiple sites. Why? Because when one site accidentally leaks your password, hackers will take your exposed password and try using it at many other popular sites on the web, including your bank and credit card websites. If you have used the same password at all those sites, then the hacker has access to all those sites as well. A good password manager allows you to use very complex and unique passwords for every site you visit, without having to memorize all those different passwords using only your brain.

Below are some really good options that we need to consider when it is time to keep our information as safe and secure as possible:

1. BitWarden
2. Dashlane
3. NordPass
4. KeePassXC
5. LessPass
6. Zoho Vault

BROWSING SAFELY ONLINE

Everyone wants to be able to go through and do their online browsing safely and without others tracking them. But in our modern world, this seems like a big dream that most of us will never get to enjoy at all. That is why we need to take some time to explore more about the best browsers and options. This effort will help keep our computers safe and let us have some fun online, without everyone knowing our business. Let's dive in and learn a little bit more about the steps and tools we can use to browse online safely.

THE BEST BROWSERS TO USE

The first thing to consider here is which browsers we would like to use when accessing the internet. Not all of these are created equal and some will provide us with a bit more security than the others. Knowing which ones will keep us safe can make a difference in how we can keep our information private. Fortunately, there are a number of private and secure browsers we can use to meet our needs as well.

Firefox is the first option on our list. This is a great browser to keep our security and privacy safe. It has a lot of privacy features and you can even set the level of privacy to Standard, Strict, or custom based on what works the best for you. This allows you to have some standard usage as needed, but you can also customize it to make it as strict as you would like. This is a unique feature that can make browsing online a lot safer for you.

The Iridium is another good browser that we can focus on. This is a secure browser that has its basis in Chromium and has been configured a bit to add in some more privacy. This is a good option if you would like to get a bit more privacy than what can be found in Chrome, but you still want to work with the Chrome extensions.

GNU IceCat browser is another one that is on our list. This is kind of a fork of Firefox that works with the GNU free software project. It is free software and still adds in some of the tweaks and the add-ons you will need to get all of the best privacy on your system. It is not as well-known as some of the others, but there is a lot to love about this one.

We can't spend time going through a discussion on what browser is the safest to use without at least a little bit of discussion about the Tor browser. Tor is a hardened version of Firefox and has been changed to work on the Tor network. The Tor browser is useful when you want to make sure that no one knows who you are or how to find you. It is good for working with browser fingerprinting and protecting you, though there are a few disadvantages. However, because of the way that the Tor network is set up to work, be aware that the speeds of doing things will be slow. This will help to protect you and will make sure that no one will find you online, but it can be a pain when you are trying to get things done quickly.

And finally, we are going to take a look at the Brave browser. This is another option that is Chromium-based and provides us with security, privacy, and fast speeds. It also has protection against browser fingerprinting and a built-in ad blocker so you know that your information will be as safe as possible as well.

PICKING THE RIGHT SETTINGS

The next thing that we need to determine if we are looking through our safety and security online is how to pick out the right settings. This will make a world of difference in whether someone is able to access our information and determine how safe things can be.

We need to first consider how strict our settings need to be for us to feel safe and secure in our work. There are different settings and various browsers that we can use. Some will significantly slow down your experience and may even block some of the things you want to look at. Finding the right balance between security and the features you prefer will be important.

Then there is the issue of working with cookies and other tracking devices. These are used by a lot of legitimate companies who just want to make sure they provide you with a top-notch experience online. But then there are some that use this just to gather a bunch of information about you and for the purpose of selling it online. If you turn off the cookies, you can keep yourself protected, but you may experience issues with some of the websites that you browse.

That is exactly what is going to happen with all of the things that we discuss in this guidebook. We have to learn how to strike the right balance between the safety and the security of our technology and the features and ease of use that you want to work with.

EXTENSIONS THAT CAN HELP YOU

For the most part, we want to avoid adding extensions to our browsers. These may sound like they are a great idea and can make your life easier. But most of them are dangerous to use and your information will be collected and used to their advantage. However, there are a few useful extensions that exist and can protect your privacy when you are online. Some of the best options to go with include:

HTTPS Everywhere ensures your connection to any website is encrypted and free from any online threats, and that all traffic back and forth is unreadable by third parties. It helps keep your browsing anonymous and your data protected, even when you are messaging others. It is going to take all of the data that you use and encrypt it, making it a lot harder for people to go on and see what you are searching for online. However, it's important to note that your data is still visible to all the parties you are giving permission to access your data while using HTTPS protocol, such as your ISP, the site you are accessing, and any third-parties already granted permission on your devices.

Privacy Cleaner is another good option that will ensure you are in control over your privacy. It can help restrict your apps and other websites when they try to get your personal information. It will start out by scanning, tracking and then controlling the apps that have permission to get your data. Then you can approve the website or the app, remove it, or report it.

Ghostery is next on the list and this extension will send you information when someone is trying to keep track of you and monitor your browsing habits. When this happens, you will be provided with a few options to ensure you have control over who will access that data. Ghostery is easy to work with and is considered an ad-blocker as well. It is an effective way to determine whether or not someone is accessing your data and provides you some good options to keep them out.

Search Lock is another great option as well, especially if you are in the habit of using search engines that are not as friendly to your privacy as others. Search Lock will make sure all your online searches stay private. Encryption is used to ensure your browsing habits and preferences are kept confidential and inaccessible from others.

HOW TO SPOT DANGEROUS EXTENSIONS

To find out whether an extension you plan to use is dangerous or safe, you have to be willing to review all the information offered and do some research. This is difficult because most of us will read a bit of the description and make our decision based on that. But these extensions must disclose imperative information that is relevant to you, such as whether they gather up data and how they use it. If you don't research their policies ahead of time, you may be downloading an extension that is dangerous and creates security weaknesses.

How do you begin your research? It is a good idea to go check out the extension developer's website. This is the most effective way to figure out whether the extension is legitimate or not. If the website looks reliable, then you are probably fine using it. But if it looks like the extension is not credible and is from someone random, then that's a red flag. It would be in your best interest to avoid using that particular extension.

Then we must also ensure we are reading the extension's description—and we mean the entire description. You need to read through everything and look for any information that is questionable, including their policy on data sharing and tracking information. Not all of the extensions that you want to use will have these details, but it is still crucial to look into.

Always pay attention to the permissions section. It will often tell you what kind of permissions will be needed to make that extension work. You should review these and understand what you are reading and what permissions you are granting. If there is a photo editing extension that needs to have access to all of the other activities or tasks you do online, then you should start questioning the reason for it.

And finally, we should check out all of the reviews to see what others have to say about their experience using the extension, whether it's positive or negative. You can't always trust one individual on these reviews. But if you read through several of these reviews and notice a general trend of negativity, then it's a sign that this isn't the best option to go with.

PROTECTING YOUR EMAIL

We send a lot of emails on a daily basis. Whether you're sending emails at work to your clients or co-workers or sending personal emails to family and friends, it is likely you'll want to make sure all that information stays secure and prevent unauthorized individuals from reading it. Even if you don't include sensitive information in the email, we often don't like the idea that someone can access what we wrote anyway. This is why we are going to take a look at some of the steps we can use to keep our emails safe. By the way, if you use Gmail, then you have already given Google permission to read all of your emails and do whatever they like with the information.

THE BEST SECURE EMAIL SERVICES

To start, we will discuss beneficial email servers that are considered the safest to work with. Most regular and free accounts are fine to use if you don't send out a lot of messages. But if you prefer your emails to always be safe and secure, and prevent others from reading them, then consider using some of the options mentioned below, which will provide us with an easy way to keep our emails private all the time.

First on the list is ProtonMail. This is a great email provider from Switzerland. You can access it on any computer from their website, and it is available through some mobile apps as well. The most important feature we must consider when describing this kind of service is whether or not someone will get a hold of your messages. Nobody is able to decrypt the messages that come with this server without your password, which is going to ensure that even if the information is lost, you will be able to know that no one can read through it. Also, because the service is located in Switzerland, you benefit from the Swiss privacy laws, and their government is much less likely to be strong-armed by other governments or law enforcement agencies into giving backdoor access to your email.

CounterMail is another viable option for those worried about email privacy. This is going to make sure that only encrypted emails are stored on this server. In addition, the servers are never going to store any of the emails on external hard drives. Instead, their data remains on CD-ROMs, which makes it easier to prevent data leaks, and if someone tries to directly mess around on the server, then the data will be lost so it is not worth the hacker's time.

Hushmail is the third option you can choose to keep your information as safe as possible. This one has been around since 1999, so we know it is secure in keeping emails private. Hushmail also ensures you are able to send out some encrypted messages to others who are on this server, or even to others who have accounts from other locations such as Outlook and Gmail if you need it.

Tutanota is the final server on our list, and it is similar to the first option (Protonmail)when it comes to security, and you are only able to access the email and the information inside if you have the right encryption key. Tutanota is a good one to use since your emails can go back and forth securely with other users. If the user needs to get to that email outside of the system, then you just need to send out a password to the recipient.

WHAT IS DISPOSABLE EMAIL?

A disposable email is a service that will help you to get rid of your spam, while still making sure that you get all of the good emails that you want, such as ones from family and friends and others you would like to hear from. With traditional options, you will have it for a little bit of time, and then the spam starts to come in. the longer that you have the email, the more the spam starts to take over.

The idea with the disposable email is that you can use it for a short period of time, and then throw it away. When you work with this address, you are not going to rely on your real email address. Instead, you will use an alias of it. Each of these aliases will be created for a mailing list or a site, and then the disposable email is going to be attached to it. The default is that all of the aliases of your real address will forward any email to that real address, just like a regular account.

As soon as you notice that some spam is coming in though, you can see a difference. Since every disposable email is given to just one site, it is easy to figure out where the source of that spam is coming from. You can then delete or disable that email and then make sure that you do not accept the spam or the messages from there at all. This can make it easier for you to go online and look for the things that you want without having your email being bombarded by a ton of email as we go.

THE WORST EMAIL SERVERS

We also need to be careful here about some of the email servers that we are using. They all promise a bunch of features and security, but they also come from some of the names we have learned about in the other parts of this guidebook. For example, Google has an email server that you can use, one that is really popular too. Do you really think that they would follow you around and sell a lot of your personal information from other apps that you use, but would stop with their email server? What about with Outlook Express from Microsoft?

It is important to be careful when using these options because they are a part of these companies who are more than willing to track you and take all of the information they can for their own needs. Even if you are sending out emails that you think are secure, this can cause a number of problems. Take your time to research some of the other options out there and find a secure email service that is not from a company that will steal your information and sell it to others.

HOW MAPS ARE HARMING YOUR SECURITY

We also need to be careful about using the maps features on some of the mobile devices that we are on. It is fine to use these on occasion in order to get a GPS or to look up where our favorite locations are. But if you do not turn these off, you do not adjust your settings or you have certain apps in place, it is possible that you are going to end up with Google, and other companies, following you.

There are many map options that seem like a good deal and it is easy to just leave them on and let us track our movements. But if you think about it, this can be really scary and dangerous. Google, Facebook, and other companies will track you and then sell this information to other parties if it makes them enough money. And if someone hacks into the system, or your own phone it would take them no time at all to track your movements and figure out where you are. Even if you are not concerned about how Google and other companies sell that information, turn off the tracking features on these maps, or don't use them at all with your phone, to make sure someone else can't follow you around.

THE GOOD AND THE BAD OF CLOUD STORAGE

Cloud services have become a really big deal and can make sure that we can find all of our documents all the time. There are situations where our computers will freeze up or maybe one just dies on us after having it for a long time. If the computer crashes, all of your documents and files may be gone for good. If you just switch to a new computer, you could spend hours trying to transfer everything over.

With the cloud, this isn't a problem. All of your documents and files and anything else important will be somewhere safe, stored on another server. No matter which computer you are on, you will be able to reach your documents without having to put in a lot of work. This keeps things secure and safe and can save a lot of headache and hassle if things go wrong.

But not all of these cloud services are as safe as they seem, and we need to take some precautions and research the ones we want to work with, or we could really harm our safety and security. And we may be handing out information that we don't mean to, and letting other companies make a profit on it. We already know through several data breaches that our data is not always as safe and secure as we would like on these cloud services, and sometimes the situation is worse than it seems. We can definitely benefit from using these services, but we must take the time to do our research before diving in.

DropBox

DropBox promises that the information you have in your folder will be safe and secure from others seeing. They state on their website that no one will be able to see or open those files unless you share the folders with them or share links to the specific files. However, it also states that like other online services, Dropbox personnel can access the file content. They can do so when it is a legal matter or when it is necessary to make sure that the system and all the features are working as designed. And they can do it when it is time to enforce the Terms of Service.

Now the first one makes sense. They can get onto your files when the police tell them too. But there are a lot of other times as well.

There are some rules that supposedly bind them and make it harder, but they have a lot of freedom to go on, even when they say there is a debugging issue to work with. This can make it a dangerous thing to work with because it is easy to see that they can get on when they want.

Google Drive and Microsoft Storage

We have already discussed how these two companies will send out information in the wrong manner. They are more than happy to go on and use information about you, even when it comes to using the cloud. If you store files on there, just be ready for some of that information to be sent out and sold to other companies as well. There are much better options that you can choose so it is often better to go with one of those.

iCloud

Apple holds onto a lot of information that you use on their systems, and that includes information that is uploaded to the cloud. They also are not fast at sending back reports of what you do on them either. While Microsoft, Google, and Twitter all sent back this information, when requested, within a few hours, it took Apple more than a week to do the same thing. When this information comes back, it also shows who you talked to and when what device you used, and more. While they don't currently hold onto information about the actual content of those messages, that is still a lot of information that we need to hold onto and be careful about when it comes to a company knowing quite a bit about us.

SHOPPING SAFELY ONLINE

Shopping online is a really big deal now. It helps to save us a lot of time because we can search on our breaks and when we are free, and we don't have to run from one store to another to get it all done. It can also make it easier to find some of the products that we want and will ensure that we get the benefit of saving money if there are two stores that offer the same product.

Shopping online can be dangerous when we want to keep our personal information secret though. Facebook often follows us and starts to track where we have shopped online. We also have to worry about someone getting on and stealing our credit card information, which grows into a really big concern when we are dealing with lots of stores that we may have shopped at in the past. Shopping safely online has to be something that we consider early on. Let's take a look at some of the steps that you can take in order to really take care of your own shopping habits to keep yourself safe online.

LOCAL WITH CASH IS KING

The number one thing that you can do here is use cash. Go directly to the store you want to shop at, pick out the items, and then pay with cash. This gives you the least amount of exposure compared to some other choices and can ensure that you are able to really make some smart decisions during this process.

With cash, no one is able to follow you or figure out where you are shopping. The money is not traceable so you can go to as many stores as you would like, and no one would be able to find you or steal your identity. You are not online, so no one is able to take a look at your browsing history and then sell that information. You get to be your own person here and that can be some great news in the process.

If you can manage it, head to the store and purchase with cash as much as you can. This will make a big difference in the success you get with protecting yourself. Even if it is not possible to do this all of the time, you will find that using cash even a few more times during the month will make a world of difference and can ensure that you will keep your money, and your own identity safe.

WHY AMAZON IS GOOD FOR ONLINE SHOPPING

Sometimes shopping in person can be inconvenient. Maybe there is something you need to purchase, but you live far away. Or you just don't have the time to run from one store to the next in the hopes of finding the item that you want. It is fine to shop online, but you need to do so in a smart and calculated manner. For example, the best and most popular place to shop online is through Amazon.

Why is Amazon such a good option? There are so many reasons. First, it has a wide selection of items you need all in one place. You won't have to worry about stopping at ten different stores in person or online and handing out your personal information that way. You get the freedom and convenience of doing all your shopping in one place, and Amazon is fairly secure so you should be safe with shopping through that platform. You only have to provide your credit card information once, or you can use the Amazon store card, and maintain your privacy bit more.

There are many great options you can use along the way to make it easier to shop online and get all of the products you want. But you do have to be careful about shopping around. The more apps and sites you use, the harder it will be to stay hidden, and more information will be provided to search engines to track you down. Amazon is a good one-stop-shop to find what you need and to get out. The reason Amazon is suggested is that it provides the most "bang for your buck." The bang refers to the products you can acquire, and the buck is your data. If you're shopping online, you will be offering up your data in some sort of capacity. Knowing that, a logical option is to keep that flow of data contained.

THINGS TO CONSIDER WITH SHIPPING

There are also a few things we need to consider when it comes to shipping items to ourselves. If you send the item directly to your home, then places like Facebook and Google now have your exact address and that can be dangerous if it gets into the wrong hands. The good news here is that there are a few options available for you to take control over your identity, and one of them is to pick an alternative way to ship the item to you. If you send it to an Amazon Locker or a PO box, then you're giving these companies a general location of where you live, but not your actual home address. That is something important to consider when you try to stay safe.

Ship to Amazon Locker

One option that you can consider if you are already using Amazon is their self-service delivery feature called Amazon Hub Locker. There are several of these located in major cities around the world, and if you live outside of one of these cities, this will keep your personal information that much safer along the way. These are simply little storage spaces where you can send your products, and then you go and pick them up. Amazon will give you all the information, and the locker number is going to change each time you use it to make it harder to track you.

Yes, it is a bit more inconvenient to use one of these compared to some of the other options out there, but it can make a world of difference as well. No one will be able to track you and even if you live in one of the big cities directly, it is not going to give away your personal information at all. That is part of the beauty of having this Amazon Locker.

Ship to a Freight Forwarder

Another option that works well is known by a few names, which includes forwarding agent, forwarder, or a freight forwarder. This is a company or a person who will be able to organize shipments for corporations or individuals to make sure that goods from a producer will make it to its destination at the right final point. These will contract with a carrier or sometimes more than one carrier to move around the goods.

The freight forwarder gives you a special address where you can send all your online shipments. Then, when the freight forwarder receives your item, they can hold it for you or ship it to any address you specify. This way, your real address is never exposed to the online merchant you purchased from.

The forwarder themselves is not going to move the goods, but they are like an expert in the logistics network and can figure out how to send from one location to another. The carrier is able to work with many methods of shipping, including railroads, trucks, airplanes, and ships to get it to the right place, and often one single shipment will use more than one of these methods to get the package to the right destination.

Because these are a bit different compared to some of the other shipping methods, and they use so many various modes of transportation, it is a lot harder to track these compared to some of the traditional methods of shipping items to ourselves. It is something to consider if you would like to keep yourself safe a bit more.

Send to Your PO Box if Possible

Perhaps you don't want to go through and head to the nearest Amazon Locker because it is three hours away or you don't like the freight forwarder option because it's an inconvenience where you live as well. The next best option is to consider a PO box. This option allows you to receive your mail at a local post office station, without a lot of hassle, like driving farther to pick up your package, but with the benefit of it not arriving directly to your home.

A PO box is fairly easy to get and the price you pay will depend on the size of the box that you get as well. You can pay per month or get a discount to have it all year. As a result, no matter what gets sent to you, you will have a safe and secure location Without having to reveal your home address.

WHY STORE MEMBERSHIPS ARE BAD

At some point or another, you have gone to the store and signed up for their membership card. Maybe you shop there regularly and feel like this is an incredible deal for you. They may give you a percentage off for your next purchase or some other reward for spending time and shopping with them. Usually, there is some incentive for you, but be aware, while this may seem like a good deal, your reward is often a lot smaller than the benefit the company is gaining from you signing up with them.

Many companies that offer similar incentives are getting a ton of information and benefits from the members. First, it helps them to bring in more customers, and often these same customers are going to spend more in order to get the points. That is something the consumer can deal with if they would like, and you can always be more mindful about the spending that you do, but it is still something to watch out for along the way as well.

The other issue, though, is that these companies are easily gathering up a lot of information about you. They know your name and address when you sign up. They may have your credit card depending on their sign-up requirements. Then they know the history of your purchases, the frequency of the items you buy, how much you spend, and so much more about your shopping habits.

You wouldn't let someone follow you around and take notes on what you purchased, how much each of the items cost, and how often you go to the store, among other factors, would you? Then why are you letting a rewards card do this to you?

Now, not all rewards cards are bad and there can be a lot of positives to working with these as well. We just need to be smart about what we are doing and learn how to do this the right way. The first step is to learn how much data you are actually handing over to the company. Whether you are comfortable with how much they take or not is your personal business, but it is still something you need to know.

THE CVS STORY

There are a lot of companies that use these rewards cards, but we are going to focus on just one example to see how this works. CVS and other supermarkets use this so much that they will offer these discount cards to provide them with a multitude of information about their shoppers. These seem to offer their customers some great bargains, with "nothing" from the client. Then when the customers use the cards, the stores can keep tabs on what has been purchased, how often you shop, and what some of your purchasing preferences are. Then this can build up a good profile of the customer so they can do customized advertisements and special offers, often from their marketing partners.

So not only is CVS able to make money by offering a few deals to their customers and then getting them to come into the store, and sometimes purchase more when they are there, the company is making money on the side too. They are selling information on your purchasing habits to other companies, and then these companies are allowed to market products to you as well.

If you enjoy using these rewards cards, then go ahead and keep using them. This isn't meant to keep you away from a good deal. But we do need to consider whether it is smart to give all of our information to a company that usually offers us groceries and other items for the house and is also making money selling our information to marketers and other companies.

DELETE ME, PLEASE

If you've done everything correctly, and you've taken all the steps above, your information still may appear online without your knowledge or consent. One of the ways you can tell is to search for your name online. You may find it, along with your address, phone number, and the names of all your relatives.

It can be frustrating when trying to remove this information and will seem impossible. But, there is a solution. There is a service called DeleteMe. The service continually scours the internet for your information, identifies the websites that are publishing your information, and automatically sends opt-out requests on your behalf. They update you quarterly on the status of your privacy and your opt-out requests. We tested this product and it worked, so DeleteMe is now recommended.

Now we need to take a bit of time to look at the world of banking and what it can do for us. Banking is a marvelous business activity in our modern world, and there is no reason that we can't use it and see great results with watching our money grow. But we also need to be careful with how we are doing this as well. if we use the wrong banks, or we are not careful with what information we give out, there could be some issues along the way. Now, let's dive deeper into the problems that can come with banking, and see why this is so important to our protection as well.

WHICH IS BETTER: CREDIT UNION OR BIG BANKS?

The first thing we need to consider when it comes to the kind of financial institution we want to use is whether to work with a big bank or a credit union. With a lot of fees that are increasing and some of the regulations that always change with banks, it is no wonder that consumers are leaving the traditional banks for credit unions instead. There are several things to consider with both of them before making a decision, but it is something we should discuss as well.

The main difference between these big banks and credit unions is that the banks are for-profit institutions while credit unions are nonprofit. This means credit unions are not going to search around to make a ton of profits for the CEO's and others who help them run. In addition, they often have lower fees, which saves you money and provides you with better customer service. Keep in mind that they do come with some higher interest rates. The big banks will often come with higher fees, but their convenience of mobile access, locations, and rewards programs are higher.

The fact that the credit union is not looking for ways to make profits, which may include taking some of your data and selling it in some big banks, can be a big benefit to switching over to them. These credit unions are also going to work with member ownership, which requires you to meet a certain set of criteria. You must either be an active member of some sort of group in your neighborhood or community, be related to someone who is a member of a credit union via their place of employment, or you could be provided with service based on the location where you live.

These are usually more local, and they are invested in the areas where they are located. They have to answer for their actions to those who are nearby, rather than being in a big office and never having to worry about how things affect the customer. This can make them really nice to work with, and you are less likely to need to deal with them selling your data, having breaches, or other issues that some of the big banks have to deal with.

CREDIT CARDS SELLING DATA

Many of the major credit cards that we use regularly are doing nothing to protect our personal information. And when they gather up some of the data, they are legally able to hold onto it forever. This makes it easy for them to take that data and sell it over and over again, giving them an advantage over others along the way.

For example, American Express and Mastercard have been caught selling the data of their customers to online advertisers. These advertisers are then able to use this data to target these consumers, including you, with lots of ads. This means that the credit card companies are able to collect fees and interest rates on you, usually at really high rates, and then they can turn around and sell that information to other people and make money on that! How low can they really get?

There are a few things that we can look at to see how prevalent this kind of problem is right now. Some information to consider when it comes to these two companies, and likely a lot of other credit cards as well, includes:

- As of 2020, Mastercard has been selling this data for more than two years.
- These companies will sell the data based on zip codes, which means they can offer their advertisers with specific areas that work better for their marketing needs. Online advertisers are then able to bid on online users from those areas and target them with some ads as needed.
- The data is anonymous and aggregated. This means that the advertisers are not able to point you out exactly, but there is still a lot of information sold about you and other customers, and that is concerning.
- Amex can sell its data as a series of models.
- eBay is even in this as well because they will sell some of the data they have for ad targeting.

One thing we should consider here is that pretty much any company who collects data right now is also going to enter into the business of selling that data and make money from it. Even if they have nothing to do with all this, and even if their customers have no idea about it at all. And since most consumers don't even realize that this is happening, organizations are able to do it under the radar and make a ton of money.

USING A BURNER CARD FROM PRIVACY.COM

We have all ordered items on the internet from some sketchy sources at some point, and we're not comfortable giving our debit or credit card information away.

Wouldn't it be ideal to have a magic button you could press that would create a one-time burner credit card to charge those purchases without it ever being traced back to you? A lot of times we end up using our credit card because there was no other option.

What most people don't understand is that every credit card company out there is double tapping you. They're making money while they are charging you for interest, plus they're billing the vendors to make everything happen, and third, on top of everything else, they sell all of your information to advertisers, who can then market back to you. And the cycle continues. They all do this, except for one institution: Privacy.com.

If you are tired of the credit card companies taking all of your information and holding onto it forever, then it is time to familiarize yourself with a burner card. This can also be a good way for you to keep theft from happening on your card at the same time. Burner cards, which are sometimes known as virtual cards, will allow you a way to minimize the amount of personally identifiable information you share with the stores that you visit. The virtual cards your bank may provide to you are clunky and hard to use, and this is where the burner cards are going to come into play.

These cards are either debit or credit that you will create through a mobile app or a website, without having a physical card attached to it. These can make online shopping a lot easier. They can be set up so that you can have a charge limit, or a maximum spend so you don't get overcharged at all. You can even lock out a merchant if you would like, so they can't charge you at all. This is great for signing up for free trials. After you sign up, you can disable the card, so the merchant can't automatically start billing you at the end of the trial period. This is great protection for times when you forget to cancel the subscription at the end of the trial.

These virtual cards are going to provide you with a new layer of protection between the merchant and the funding source. They will pass any of the transactions right to the funding source. These cards offer a buffer in case some of the companies you use get breached. Since the card number is different for every vendor, this keeps you safe and secure. For example, if your account at an online store gets hacked, and your credit card is exposed, the thief cannot use that card number at any other vendor. It won't work. Privacy.com ensures that the card will only work for one vendor, and they give you a new card number for every online store at which you shop.

And since that information is hard to tie back to you, it gets even harder for someone to trace your purchases and keep up with where you are and what you are doing along the way. This can keep your information safer and easier to work with. Even your own bank won't know what you've been purchasing because you can set a fake description for all your purchases, and this description is what will show on your bank statement.

THE ARGUMENT FOR NOT CARD CUTTING

As we go through some of this information, you may feel like it is best to just take those credit cards and cut them up. If you have credit cards that are only a temptation for you and don't provide you with any beneficial information at all, then it is time to cut them. Despite this, there are a few good reasons to work with a credit card, and learning how to use it wisely can be a good thing as well.

First, if you are able to gain some good rewards from these, then it may be worth it. These need to be good rewards, though. If it takes you twenty years of regular spending before you can even use the rewards or get enough to make it worth your time, then cut those cards up. If your normal spending makes sense for the rewards you will get, then go ahead and do that. If you still want to cut them up to avoid any problems and hassles, find out what it will take to save your travel rewards and other benefits, or use them, ahead of time.

Sometimes, it is also nice to have these credit cards around in case of an emergency or as a convenience. It is much more convenient to pull out a card and use that instantly for your needs rather than having to stop by the bank and grab cash before you have to go to the store. These are legitimate reasons, but maybe consider some ways you can cut back on using credit cards and only use them when necessary rather than frequently.

IS PAYPAL SAFE?

Many people use PayPal because it is a method that is supposed to keep their personal information safe and protect sensitive information. This has become a very popular site to use because of some of the consumer protections it puts in place, but because of this popularity, it has also become a major playground for thieves to come in and cause some problems.

You have to take extra precautions to make sure someone isn't able to access and take your information and use it to their advantage. For example, it is usually not recommended that you add in your banking or your debit card information. This may seem easier in some cases. But if a hacker is able to get onto the system and cause some damage, then they could clear out your whole account, and you are out of luck in the process. Plus, the credit card is going to offer you another level of protection because the money isn't in an account yet, and most credit cards offer you some extra safeguarding along the way. Or, even better, you can use one of the burner cards to make this work a bit better.

This is another benefit of still using your credit card, though you should be careful with this one. According to federal law, if you go and file a dispute with the issuer of your credit card, it is going to ask PayPal to prove that the transaction was legitimate or not. If PayPal is unable to confirm, then they are on the hook with your bank rather than you. This provides PayPal with some more incentive to be careful with the transactions that they complete.

Also, be careful with some of the links you receive from PayPal. Many times, these may not be from PayPal, which alone should be concerning that someone has been able to get your email and then send you a spoof connected to your PayPal email address. Even if the message appears it came from PayPal and has the logo and other convincing details, you should not tap on the link included in the emails or you could give your information away from a hacker.

For the most part, working with PayPal is reasonably safe. But you still need to be careful about the amount of details you give. Even without issues from PayPal, there are still a lot of people who would like to get on and steal all of your information.

SHOULD I USE BITCOIN?

Bitcoin is an alternate currency that is only available to use online. You can't print it off and use it at traditional stores. It also doesn't have a central government in charge of it. This is a blessing because it keeps your information secret and away from others. But it is also a challenge because no one is regulating the market, so things can go wrong.

A growing number of stores online accept Bitcoin and other cryptocurrencies as they are called. You can go through and choose to pay with this, just like you would with PayPal and your credit card. The difference is that these are not linked back to your name. They are simply linked back to your wallet, which has a unique alpha/numeric code with it. No one who traces back the bitcoin to your wallet will be able to tell the name, or anything else, about the person who owns that wallet.

This can make it a lot safer to shop and do things online because people will not be able to come back and figure out who you are. You have to set it up, which is pretty easy through a few exchange sites, and then work from there. And it is a whole lot safer to work with than your credit card or some of the other methods out there because it is impossible to track and utilize in that manner.

There are a few things to note about Bitcoin and other cryptocurrencies before you try to use it, though. First, remember that while this is a helpful method for a lot of things, you also need to realize that it is not regulated. This means that the price can go up and down like crazy, and no one is there to keep it safe and secure. This can be a big issue if you put in some money and then the price of Bitcoin drops, causing you to be without any money. And if something else goes wrong with the system, you have no one to speak with to resolve issues. Also, if you lose bitcoin, it's like losing cash. There will be no bank to complain to or any real way to get it back.

THE SEARCH ENGINE YOU ULTIMATELY DECIDE TO WORK WITH is going to be imperative. It can make the difference between keeping your information safe and having a company take those details and use it for their advantage. You need to decide whether you want the perks and the features, or your own privacy in some cases, but that can be a personal decision based on your own needs. Some of the search engines to consider are:

DUCKDUCKGO

This is one of the best search engines that you are able to go with, especially when you are focusing on keeping your privacy safe. While some of the other options may beat it out on occasion for providing some better searchers, this one can hold its own, without having to take all of your data, track you, and do some of the other negative things we've discussed previously along the way.

DuckDuckGo is focused on protecting the consumer's privacy, and it is going to work as much as possible to avoid the filter bubble that comes with providing personalized search results. So, when you use it, the results are not going to be customized like they can with other options, but it is still going to help you to not have something following you around and collecting all of your information.

This company can distinguish itself from other search engines because it is not going to profile its users. This means that when you use DuckDuckGo, you will see the same results show up on the screen as all other users if they were to type in the same search terms. This is great news for protecting your privacy and making sure your details are kept safe. It is still going to provide you with some good results because it has more than 400 sources to provide you information, including Bing, Yandex, and its own kind of web crawler and more.

STARTPAGE

If you are still fond of the search results that Google provides you, but you are looking to gain a bit more privacy in the process, then Startpage is the option to go with. When you submit a search through this one, the Startpage search engine is going to submit a search to Google, which in turn will give you the results. But what will be visible to Google is that Startpage is sending in these search requests and therefore will not be tracked back to you.

This page can discard all of the information that would tie back to you. It also won't work with cookies, will get rid of some IP addresses, and it won't keep a record of the searches that are done. This method allows you to get the results you want without having someone tracking you or storing all of the information for their own needs.

IXQUICK

This is one of the main search engines from the same company that brings us the Startpage from above. Unlike that one though, this search engine is going to provide us with results from more than one source. This can be bad or good, depending on the kinds of results you'd like or whether you want to retrieve outcomes from Google or not. This will have a similar design as Startpage so you can decide which one works the best for you.

BLEKKO

You will find that Blekko is not going to go quite as far as the other options we have talked about previously when it comes to your privacy and your security, but you will still find that it is a big improvement over Bing and Google, so that is a good thing. Blekko is going to log some information about you, but it is deleted within two days at the most. On the other side of things, Google is going to store your information for nine months and then instead of deleting it, the company will anonymize it without actually erasing the information so it can be available forever.

GOOGLE, BING, AND MORE

We discussed a bit earlier in this guidebook why Google and Bing are options that we can use, but we have to be careful about it. These companies are more than willing to take your search history, your emails, and more, and then use that data to uncover more information about you. They will then turn around and either use that data for some of their own products, or they will use it to sell to other marketers and advertisers who will then use it as they wish.

This is why we need to be mindful about using these companies before they take our data and cause more problems along the way. This doesn't mean that we can never use them, though. Their services do provide some benefits, such as better search results than some of the others. And Bing even offers incentives like gift cards and more if you search with them. For some, this is worth their time and energy to use, even if the company is taking some of their information.

It has also been shown that these companies will tailor search results based on your data, such as location, previous search history, and more! This means that you may not be getting the best information possible for what you're searching. They may show results that are sponsored or that are based on what they think you're going to "buy" versus what you are intending to search.

You have to decide whether safety and security and withholding your personal information is more important than accessing features for convenience. There isn't a wrong answer here, but it is still crucial to at least be aware that when you take those incentives and rewards, the company may be taking more information than it seems on the surface. If you know this and are comfortable with it, then that is fine as well.

THE NEAT THING IS THAT THERE IS SOMETHING WE CAN DO here. Not everything has to rely on someone else coming in or using some other services to keep our information safe and secure. We can also work on a few DIY (Do It Yourself) projects and make sure that no one else can get into our information or track us along the way. Some of the options that we are able to utilize include:

HOW TO SET UP A PERSONAL CLOUD

We talked earlier about how working with a regular cloud can be a great idea, but sometimes it leaves us wide open to an attack of some kind. Being able to put our information on hold, and place it somewhere safe, without storing it with a company that will use it however they want, can be an ideal solution. And that is why we are going to look at the steps to set up our own cloud for personal use.

In order to activate and begin using your new cloud, you need to add in a hard drive to your home network, which is known as a

NAS, or Network Attached Storage device. Fortunately, there are already a lot of products out there that can do this and are full of all the hardware and software that is needed to make this happen. It is important to have a bit of basic knowledge so you can ensure that you can both customize and connect it to the other devices, but there are a few things you should consider.

First, make sure you come up with a reasonable estimation of giga-bytes of data you will be using. It is typically best practice to think of how much you need and then double it to ensure you have enough to grow. Keep in mind that if you get 500GB of data, you can store 8,500 hours of music, 155,000 pictures, and 500 hours of video as a reference here. Then you need to consider which devices you would like to use to access that cloud. Are you just going to work with one device or many? That will make a differ-ence on what you will use here. And then make sure that the device you pick out will be compatible with the operating system you plan to use.

When you have all this in mind, and you have your NAS device, it is time to set it all up. The steps required to make this happen includes:

1. Remove the NAS drive from the box it came with and then put it with a network node or a router.
2. Turn it on.
3. Start up the software that came with it on your computer. It is likely that you will need to run some installation software first to get the best results.
4. Power up the program and carefully follow a few prompts to choose the IP address. Make sure that before doing this, you can give the hard drive a name and take advantage of other customization options, such as having

control over the settings you apply to the power system in your device.

5. Next, make sure you are certain of what files you would like to put on this personal cloud. You can also choose how often these files will be backed up.
6. Create the information to log in. This is important if you want to sync with your other devices in order to get that information.
7. Use your personal login information to access your cloud and other devices to make sure that this is working. You may need to add some software there as well to make it work.

And that is all there is to it. It is a simple process, but it does take a few more steps to be successful. And the cost upfront is usually a bit more, though this goes down over time compared to others. It is a good way to make sure that your data is always backed up and safe, without having to trust another company to ensure someone else won't get your information.

RASPBERRY PI

Raspberry Pi is one of the best options to use if you want to learn about computer science and all it entails without having to be technical. This was a programming language, with a computer board designed to help teach students how to work with technology. This is good news for you because it means you can work on setting up a few security parts on your own without having to spend years in school.

PI-HOLE TO BLOCK ADS AND MALICIOUS SITES

As we mentioned a little bit before, the pi-hole is going to be a kind of filter that will be able to catch most ad traffic before it can be loaded up onto your browser. This is going to make your browser faster because it eliminates ads from being loaded, and also eliminates the extra code required to deliver the ads. You don't have to spend a lot of money to do this, though, because you can create one of your own with the steps we will talk about now.

First, we need to purchase our own Raspberry Pi 3 and make sure it is added to your network. These can be less than $50 in most cases, which is not so bad. For an even cheaper and smaller alternative, the Pi-Hole can be operated on a Pi Zero. Once you have the device, you need to connect it right to the network that you would like the ads blocked on. To do this, plug one end of an Ethernet cable into the back of the Pi and then have the other one in the router. Then wait to see the status light show up so that you know the Pi is connected.

When this is done, it is time to install the operating system on your Pi device. To do this, you can go and visit the Raspberry Pi website. There are a few options, but the one that we want to use to make this work well is Raspbian Buster with Pixel. When this has finished, you can install it on the micro SD card that you plan to use with the device. Insert this SD card into the Pi device before restarting.

When the Pi comes back on, you can take a moment to identify the Pi on your network. You can open the control panel for the router by typing in the internal IP into Google. It is a bit different for each router, but this can be a simple process to go through. Once you have made it to this control panel, you need to go to the list of connected devices and find the IP that goes with your Pi device.

Now we need to connect and configure the Pi device so that it works well with the Pi-hole that we want to use. You can then download the program known as Putty. Put the IP of the Pi into the hostname and then click to open it. Once it is connected, you need to go through and run a set of commands. These commands are simple to work with, and you can type the following into your Pi CMD window:

```
Curl — SSL https://install.pi-hole.net |bash|
```

This will make sure we are able to install the software we need for this program to work. The last thing we need is to set this as the active DNS server through the router that you are working with. This is a bit different for all routers, but you need to first find the section of the control panel of the router where we are able to input the static DNS server. While there, we can type in the IP that comes with the device and make sure to set it at the DNS server that is active. When this is complete, you will be able to access the interface for the web and log into it, viewing the total ads that are blocked, and even some of the settings of the configuration. If you would like to connect to this interface, just type the following: pi-hole/admin.

And that is all there is to this process. You now have your own Pi-hole set up through the Raspberry Pi device, and you can block all the ads that you would like. This is a lot cheaper to work with than a lot of the other devices and options out there, but it can provide you with some really good choices when it's time to keep your information safe.

SET UP A PRIVATE DNS SERVICE

If you like all the benefits that come with a Pi-hole but don't want the hassle of setting up and managing a hardware solution, then you're going to love the idea of using a private DNS service like NextDNS.

They are true supporters of net neutrality and internet privacy and believe that unencrypted DNS resolvers operated by Internet Service Providers (ISPs) are detrimental to those two principles. Alternative solutions like Cloudflare DNS or Google DNS are great, but we think more actors, like NextDNS, need to step up and provide alternative services to avoid the centralization of powers.

NextDNS offers all the functionality of the Pi-hole, but it is managed through a website and is super-fast. You can set up your computer, or other individual devices to route all your domain name lookups through NextDNS so that your ISP does not know where you're browsing. And NextDNS will keep your activity private. They promise that they do not (and will never) sell, license, sub-license, or share any of the data submitted directly or indirectly by users with any person or entity. And when the service comes into contact with user data that shall not be logged, it is discarded as quickly as possible. If not explicitly requested by the user, no data is logged. They also protect users from privacy exposure to other services that they must interact with to operate correctly. All these aspects add up to better privacy for you.

SECURING A ROUTER

Another thing that we need to consider while we are going through this is how to secure your own router. Having a good router in place and making sure that no one is able to come through and steal information about your computer and your network without your knowledge, is important. And sometimes picking out your own router, rather than using the one from the internet provider you work with, can make things a lot safer over-all. Let's take a look at how to make this happen and what steps we can take to select an effective router for our needs.

WHAT MODEL TO BUY

The model you want to use will depend on what you would like to do with the process and what kind of security you prefer. Some-times, it also depends on the amount of money you're willing to pay as well. Some of the best models you can try out include:

1. Linksys WRT 3200 ACM router. This is a good choice when it comes to picking out a VPN (Virtual Private Network) router. The design doesn't include anything that you don't need, and it is versatile and has a lot of power so you can use it for VPN and many other options. It is easy to install some DD-WRT firmware that is compatible with VPN, and there are three bands and four antennae in these to make sure that you can get lots of speeds on your network. There are also four Ethernet ports to hook into it, which will make it easier to use, even if you don't plan to work with VPN.

2. Asus RT-AC86U. This is an ideal one for those who are familiar with Asus and some of the products that are centered around games. Even if you haven't used it before, it is a lot of fun and can provide you with some of the resources you need to get things done. This one works well for VPN, even without some of the gaming done on it. The features will make it a fast performer that won't make the speeds of your internet drop as much when you turn on the VPN, compared to some of the other options. It is also possible to add on a bit of firmware from other companies to make sure you get the most protection possible.

3. D-link DIR-885L/R router. If you would like to work with a router that is dependable and mid-range, and you can have some good speed and lots of features for gaming, along with a good range in Wi-Fi, then this is the router you want to work with. This particular router will come with a wide selection of ports, and the user interface to set it up and configure it is easy to use, even for beginners. It also has its own firmware, which adds in some of the power and flexibility we need, and you can easily add some customizations to make it work even better.

4. **Netgear Nighthawk X4S VDSL/ADSL Modem Router:** If there was a fashion contest for routers, then this is the one that would win. It has a black finish that is solid and is complemented with four antennas for easy access. It is really fast and has a duo of USB ports that come with an eSATA connector as well. The real centerpiece to work with here is the VDSL 2 modem that is built into it, which means you will not have to purchase or use one separately. And the software that comes with it helps you to hook up and keep more than one device as safe as possible in the same home.

5. **ExpressVPN:** The final option we will look into is known as the ExpressVPN. This is going to offer an iPad app that is native, works with iOS 8 and higher, and will make it so that you just need to click on it once to get it connected. The security is some of the best and has all the encryption you need. The VPN on this router will not log any of the data about your traffic, your DNS queries, or anything else someone can use to figure out who the user is.

These are just a few of the options we can choose when it comes to picking out a router that is safe and secure to use. You can do some research and see if other options will provide you a good balance between price point and the security you are looking for all in one.

HOW TO SET UP YOUR VPN ROUTER

The first option you can use is to pick out one of the routers listed above. These all have the VPN on them and will help to protect you from the traffic that comes in and will make it harder for others to know who you are and what you are doing when you are online. This method is usually a bit easier to work with, and it is the option most people will choose. Since each router will be a bit different, you should read through the instructions to see what you need to do to take that device and get it hooked up to your internet and ensure your traffic is safe.

It is possible in some cases to use a VPN server software on your own computer and have that protect your traffic instead. This takes a bit more work, but it can be a good way to keep you safe. You will want to use a device or a computer you can keep on all the time, rather than a desktop PC that is going to turn off when you leave your home, or this will not work. The good news is that Apple's Server app and Windows will both make it easier to build up this VPN server as you would like, and Windows even has it set up so you can host the built-in VPNs.

If you want to avoid Windows and Apple, you can work with a VPN server that is from a third-party instead. A good option is OpenVPN. These servers are available and can work with all operating systems, so you won't have to make some changes to this if you don't want to. All that has to happen here is to forward the right ports from your router to the computer that is running the software on the server.

Another option we can work with here is taking your own dedicated VPN device and using this. Remember that Raspberry Pi we talked about before? You can use this and then install the OpenVPN server software, which will turn that Raspberry Pi into your own VPN server in no time. Or you can go through the process to install other server software onto the Raspberry Pi if you would like and get it to be a multi-purpose server that does all the work you want in no time.

No matter which method you choose, you should double-check that there is some firmware attached to it as well. This will add an extra layer of protection that makes it easier to keep others out. You do not want to let advertisers and others get into your system and start wreaking a bunch of havoc, so having the firmware and the VPN together can be a great way to keep attackers out and away from you.

CONSIDERING ANONABOX

One option you are able to take a look at when picking a router that can protect your privacy is known as Anonabox. This is a device from Linux that is going to route all of the traffic coming to you from the internet through the Tor network. This is going to provide you with the power of the Tor network without having to worry about having extra software you have to download and use.

This is actually the first router available commercially that can be embedded with Tor, and all of the software we use is open-sourced. You can call this a cloaking device because it is not only responsible for scrambling your location and the activity online, but it will allow someone to get access to the web without censorship, and in places where some sites on the internet are blocked.

One thing to keep in mind here is that when you use this method, it is going to slow down your speed. This is a feature that is common with Tor because the way you connect is a bit different. This is normal and will ensure your information stays safe and secure, and no one can track you. But it can be a bit annoying if you are not careful about how you do this.

Working with this box is not a requirement in order to keep things safe, but it is going to make a big difference in how much time you can save along the way. The other methods can work as well, but this one comes with Tor, which allows us to make some choices on the websites that we are able to work with on this kind of network. It depends on how much security and safe access you would like to have online.

ONE MORE CONCEPT WE NEED TO TALK ABOUT BEFORE moving on is configuring our LAN and devices. These are all important to ensure you are keeping people out and that you are a bit harder to find, even if you spend some time online.

Before we dive too much into this one, we need to take a look at what a LAN is all about. A LAN stands for Local Area Network and it is basically a collection of devices that can connect with one another in one physical location whether it is your home, an office, or a building. You can have a small LAN, but you can also have a large one. It is possible to have one that has thousands of devices and users, but it is also possible to have just one device in your home network.

The LAN will include all of the components of a network, from the routers, switches, access points, and cables, that will enable a device to connect back to the web servers, internal servers, and some other LANs via wide area networks. The benefits of working with this are the same as those for any group of devices that are networked together. The devices are then able to use the same internet connection, share the files with each other, print to one printer that is shared and can be accessed and sometimes controlled by one another.

With this in mind, we need to take some time to look at the best methods we can use to handle some of these LANs and to make sure that we are using them in the best way possible. Let's dive in and see how we can work with them.

NO SSID BROADCAST

One thing you can work on to keep yourself safe is to turn off the SSID broadcast that shows up, or in other words, the name of your Wi-Fi network. This is a goldmine for a lot of companies who search for it, but it is going to make things very hard for you when you try to hide, and you don't want the company to be able to know your location. When the SSID is broadcasting, companies can take a look at it, compile a list of network IDs and then they can geolocate them on a map and see where their customers are. This means that if your SSID is broadcasting, the company can see where you are, where you are in location to others, where you go to, and so much more.

To start, we need to know what the SSID (otherwise known as the service set identifier) broadcast is all about. This is essentially the name assigned to your wireless network. This illustrates the way your router can transmit its own name to nearby devices. The main function here is to make sure your network is easy to access and visible, which sounds like a great idea until a company wants to use this against you. The SSID by default will usually include the brand name of the device, but you can go through and change this as well.

The SSID is going to broadcast the signal on its own. You have to go through and change some of the router settings to disable the

SSID, or you can go back and reverse this if you would like to turn it back on. The good news is that this is pretty easy to do, and you won't have to spend hours on it.

First, you can just open up the control panel of your router, which is easy to do through a web browser. Then type in the IP of the router. If you are unsure about where this is, you can look up the instruction manual for your router and look there. Add this to the address field before submitting. Then it is time to enter the password and username. If you did not already change it, then they are the defaults provided in the manual. This is a great time to change the username and password if you have not done so already.

Disabling this is a great way to make sure that the name of your network is invisible to others. However, this is not going to hide the network, just the name of it. You will not be able to hide the activities of the router, but it will make it harder for the companies to find you and use it against you. Keep in mind that with the network invisible to wireless devices, connecting can be a bit harder as well, so be mindful if you are thinking about hiding the network as well.

It is not necessary to hide the SSID if you don't want to go through the work and the hassle of it. But it is an added layer of protection that makes it harder for someone else to figure out where you are and what you are doing online. It is one of the best ways to keep your name hidden, and even if they can see your network, it is going to be a lot harder for them to pinpoint you and figure out what you are doing all the time.

TURN THE LOCATIONS OFF YOUR DEVICES

Many devices have an automatic feature attached to them that lets others know their location. Depending on the device you are using, the software that is on it, the apps you like to use and more, there is a varying degree of how specific this is going to be. Some may know the region or the state you are in, some may know which city or town. And some are so specific that they know where you ate for lunch that day.

The more specific these locations are, the more dangerous it can be. This is advantageous for marketers and advertisers because they can follow you and figure out what you are doing all the time. But even if that doesn't bother you as much, think about how you would feel if a hacker or someone else got on and could see where you were all the time? Maybe that is creepy enough to convince you to turn off the location setting on your devices.

Don't just do this on one device, though. It is best to go through and do this on all devices. The more that you can limit where others will see you and your location, the better. There are several options you can choose and settings that will allow you to turn this off as well. Any time you add in new apps or software, make sure to check and turn off any of the location tracking.

HOW DNS CAN KEEP US SAFE

Privacy is so important, which is why we have spent so much time on it in this guidebook so far. But there are so many other parts that we need to worry about here to make sure we can really keep our information as safe and secure as possible. The DNS, or the Domain Name System, is something that we can use to make it harder for others to find and track us, as long as we know how to use it.

Every domain name (i.e., Google.com) has a number behind it. That number is called the IP address. We can think of DNS as a phone directory that is able to match some memorable name like

Google.com, to a set of numbers (the IP address.) When you enter a website in your browser, you are sending a request to a DNS resolver that will look up the IP address of that website. It is then able to form that connection and then the function is done.

This sounds pretty simple, but we run into some issues when it comes to privacy. By nature, this service is going to come up with a record of all the addresses that you have entered and searched for before. This means that whoever is able to run that server can see which sites you visited in the past. As most of these servers are run by a for-profit company or some ISPs, the data found here is going to provide them with a ton of information they can then sell to their marketers.

There are a few options we can use that will help to prevent these issues. And one of the best is known as 1.1.1.1 from Cloudflare. It is a great option that almost seems too good to be true. Yes, with this one, you are still going to send out those web address requests you did in the past and it will go to the right server, and usually, that server is to a for-profit company. But this DNS service is going to make it a bit different in a sense that all the searches you do with it will not be written down or recorded. And all the logs will be deleted after 24 hours so that no one is able to come through and use it against you.

This is a great option if you want to make sure that the servers you work with are not able to take your information and use it against you. As a result, you get to use that server, look up anything you would like and be confident that your website visit records are not being sold away for profit. This can save you a lot of worries and can protect your privacy in the process.

Now, setting up a computer to use this kind of DNS, or some of the other options like NextDNS and OpenDNS, is a bit more complicated. But you only have to go through the process one time to get it all set up, and then nothing is needed again. And the best part is that you don't even need to install it at all. You will have to go through and have the right superuser or administrator privileges, but that is all.

ROUTER SETTINGS TO KEEP YOU SAFE

One of the inevitable problems with using the internet is that there really isn't a good security standard for it. This means we are likely to go out and purchase thermostats, speakers, cameras and more and assume our buying activities are safe and secure. When in reality they are not, and we are setting ourselves up to have some issues along the way. Fortunately, there are a few router settings and other options we can use in order to make our network safe and ensure that we are able to keep the hackers out, and all of our information safe.

AUTOMATIC UPDATES

When your router gets an update, it is likely you won't even realize it. And newer routers are able to do this without you doing any work. If the process is not automatic, then you have to go through and do this on your own once every three months to keep online activities safe.

To help you get to the admin page of your router, you will need the admin password and the IP address. You can look at the user guide of your router for these details. There are also a few sites that can help you to find these if your router is a bit older and you are not able to find it. When you have found this admin page, then go to the "advanced" part of it and look to see if there are any updates to the firmware. If this is there, then download the updates. And if you have a chance, then you should enable your router to do these updates automatically on its own.

SET UP SOME STRONGER ENCRYPTION

Most routers will have some kind of encryption by default. If you have to enter a password just to connect, then this is already there. But that doesn't mean that we are done here yet. There are different encryption types that work on your Wi-Fi, and some are much weaker and easier to hack than the others.

The method that is the most popular and the most secure right now is WPA3 or Wi-Fi Protected Access 3. This standard is more than ten years old, but it is the newest option so make sure that any routers you pick out will support this. To check out what kind of encryption is found on your router, you need to go back to the admin menu for the router. You should be able to find this under the Security or the Wireless menu.

If the router that you are using is not set up to work with WPA3, then the next best option is the WPA2-PSK AES. If you have some of the older networks, then this is the one you will need to use. But it is best to get it up to date, and the higher the encryption, the better it will keep the hackers out.

BUILD IN A FIREWALL

One of the best tools for security you can use is a router that has a firewall in it. Nearly all of the routers that have been made in the past ten years will have some form of this firewall in it, which is good news. You will find that not all of the routers out there have their firewall labeled the same. You will often find this under some of the advanced settings of your router, like NAT filtering, port filtering, port forwarding, or something else.

These are good settings to look at, though, because they will allow you to tweak some of the incoming and the outgoing data ports and can protect them a bit from outsiders. But you do need to be careful with these settings. The default firewall that is there will usually be enough, and if you do not configure the ports well, it can either make it easier for the hackers to get on and steal your information, or it can make it hard for you to get online. If you do try to mess with this and make a mistake, talking to your internet provider is the best option because they can tell you which port settings are the ideal for your needs.

OPTIMIZED QUAD9 DNS SETTINGS

Another thing that we need to look at here to see if we can stay safe and secure is the Quad9 Domain Name System service. This is something that is maintained by some of the biggest advocates of cybersecurity, including the Global Cyber Alliance and IBM. Once set as the service of DNS that you want to use, every time that you click on a link online, this is going to check the site to see if it is a threat or not.

This is a good way to make sure that your data and your computer will stay safe. There are so many websites out there, and many of them are safe to use. And then there are those that seem safe and good to use, but they really are not. If you are not careful, a hacker can get on and take all of your information. That is where this setting is going to come in handy. It is able to look through a really large database, which includes more than 40 billion images and web pages that are already analyzed and can tell you whether something is safe and secure to use.

DON'T ALLOW FOR REMOTE ACCESS

Remote access is something that many of us have been able to use in the past, but it is best if we learn how to keep that turned off. If someone does it once and doesn't close all of the backdoors that come with it, then we are going to end up with some trouble along the way and the hackers will be able to get on as well. If you have ever had a time when a technician was able to take control of your computer while you talked to them on the phone, then you are familiar with what this remote access is all about and how it is easy to use.

Hackers and scammers will find that this remote access is a simple way for them to get onto a home network. Remote desktop management is one of the pillars of several flaws of security that is found with a Windows computer. When you are looking at your router, it is better if you can just turn off these settings without allowing any access. This is something we can find under the heading of "Remote Administration" in the router settings.

In addition, even if you go through and do these steps, there is still the step of locking down the devices that can access the internet. You can make sure no one is able to get online or do things you don't approve of and keep them from having remote access to your devices from anywhere in the world.

9 / BEST PRACTICES

To finish this guidebook, we need to take a look at some of the best practices we can follow, specifically the ones that will make sure we are as safe as possible. It is hard to keep all of the tracking away from us, especially in this modern world, but there are some steps we can use that will make it at least a little bit difficult on those who try it. Let's take a look at some of the options we can use to make sure we are safe and secure, and that no one will be able to steal our information and sell it for profit.

CONSIDER: DO I REALLY NEED THE PRODUCT OR SERVICE?

The first thing we need to consider here is whether we actually need a product or a service. This is something we should be asking to start with because it can be so great for our budget and making our money stretch a bit further. But it is also something good that will help to keep us protected. And when it is time to order that product online, it is definitely something we must consider to keep our personal information safe.

It is so easy to go online and order items. Then we take out the credit card (or even worse, we have that card saved on the website that we are ordering from), and then the item is on its way. The more times we utilize our credit cards and shop online, the more data that these companies can use against us, and the more dangerous it can be. This doesn't mean we have to cut out shopping online completely. But we do need to be more cautious about how many products we decide to purchase online.

First, decide if you really need that item or not. If you don't, then it is time to put the card away and not purchase it at all. If you do need the item for one reason or another, consider whether you are able to go somewhere local and pay in cash, or even if you can use a burner credit card. This will make it so much easier to keep your data safe and sound.

HOW TO TURN OFF DATA SHARING

We spent some time talking about how Facebook and other companies are able to take our data and use it in any manner they want. The good news here is that we do get some control over this, and we do get some say in how this is supposed to work along the way. it is possible to go through some of these sites and turn off the data sharing. We are going to look at how to make this happen with three of the popular ones, Google, Facebook, and Twitter, but the process is similar on many other sites, and you should consider doing the same thing to keep you safe.

GOOGLE

It is possible to go through and edit the data sharing with Google. They do make it pretty simple, but you have to be careful and make sure you actually do this. To change the settings you have for data sharing with Google, first sign into your Google account page. Then you can click on the Admin button and select "Manage your Google Account." Then select "Manage your Data & Personalization." Edit the settings that you would like and click on Save to get it all in one place.

You may also have to go through and repeat some of the same steps on other apps you use through Google to make sure they stop going after you completely. This can take a lot of time, especially if you use a lot of the programs and options from Google, so be prepared for that along the way.

FACEBOOK

Now let's take a look at how we can turn off this data sharing on Facebook. First, we need to make sure we are logged into our Facebook page, and then we can go to our App settings page. It is possible to go there manually by typing in Settings Menu, and then Apps. When we get to this point, we can click on the Edit button, which we can find under Apps, Websites, and Plugins. From there, click on the Disable Platform.

If this is too much, then there is another set we can use. This is one that allows us to limit the personal information that is accessible to apps, which are used by others. The default of Facebook and even Instagram is that other people who can see your information will then be able to bring it over with them any time that they use their apps, and that makes it available to those apps as well. This is something we should consider limiting as well.

To do this, we need to get back to the same page we were before and then click the Edit button, which is under "Apps Others Use." Then we can go through and uncheck the types of information that you would like to prevent other apps from using. It is likely that you will want to uncheck all of the boxes as you go along.

These steps will keep you safe with both Facebook and Instagram, and it is possible that it will keep you safe through a few other apps and extensions that work with Facebook. It is simple to use, but we have to make sure we take the steps to turn this off and keep ourselves safe.

Facebook also keeps track of everywhere you've been when you are NOT on Facebook. How do they do this? Other websites have agreed to tell Facebook what you are doing when you're away from the social media site in exchange for the opportunity to access and use Facebook's advertising platform.

To see what Facebook knows about where you've been on the web, go to https://www.facebook.com/off_facebook_activity. Then, click "Manage Your Off-Facebook Activity.'" You will see a list of all the websites that have willingly exposed your browsing activity to Facebook, so that Facebook may continue to track you even after you leave Facebook.

The first thing you can do is erase these records by clicking the "Clear History" button on that page. But if you want to prevent Facebook from continuing this dubious behavior, you'll need to click "Manage Future Activity" and then turn this feature off.

TWITTER

Twitter will collect your personal data to help with targeted advertising, and then they will share that data with some other companies if it chooses. You do have a say in whether they collect all that data, and it is possible to turn off the settings. Some of the steps you can take to turn off these settings and keep yourself safe include:

1. Go to the Personalization and Data settings website that comes with Twitter.
2. When you are there, you can click on the button that says Disable. This will stop all of the data that is collected for advertising.
3. Make sure to click on Save changes or it will not stick, and Twitter will continue to use your information.
4. Click "Yes, I'm sure" when it asks to finish the process.

SHOPPING LOCAL AND WITH CASH

As we mentioned before, cash is king, and it is something that we really should utilize more. This is not only a really good budgeting tool that will make sure you watch your money more, but it is a lot harder for a hacker to go and steal your money if the cash is in your pocket. And it is harder for stores and other locations to track you and then sell that data and information to others.

While you are shopping around with cash, you should also consider taking some time to shop local. Local stores are going to include your neighbors and others who are invested in your community as well. And most of them are not going to take your data and try to sell it to someone else. This makes them a lot more secure to work with, and you won't have to worry about your data disappearing and being used against you. As much as you can, shop local and use cash, and you will find that your privacy is protected a whole lot more.

USE THE BURNER CREDIT CARDS

We took some time to talk about these burner credit cards earlier and how great they can be for helping you to keep your information safe. If you plan to use online shopping and you want to do this regularly, then these burner cards are going to be the best option for you. Credit cards can offer a ton of protection if you use them well, but they are also really good for hackers to take and use on their own. And by the time you catch what is going on, you are in trouble and may not be able to fight it along the way.

These burner cards can make it a bit easier to take the control back and to make it harder for websites to store your information and use it against you. Several sites are good for providing you with these burner cards if that is the route you would like to take. Since they are more secure, make a new burner card for each merchant so you aren't using the same one, and you are able to put limits on how much can be used. These are a whole lot safer compared to using your traditional credit card along the way.

Currently, the only company we recommend for burner credit cards is Privacy.com.

CONSIDER TWO-FACTOR AUTHENTICATION

This is not always possible, but if it is, then you need to work with something known as two-factor authentication. Most companies and websites just have one factor. You put in your username and your password, and that is it. That is just one thing blocking a hacker or someone else from getting your information. And while it may be simple, it is going to also make it easier for a hacker to come in and use it as well.

With the two-factor authentication, we add in another level here. This one allows us to have a regular username and password, and then there is a second level. This could be a pin that is required after the username and password are authenticated, or a finger-print or something else. If the person doesn't have both, then they are not able to get onto the account that is protected. This is just another level of protection that will make it easier for you to stay safe and to keep the hackers out.

As we mentioned, this is not possible on all accounts, but if you have some that offer the two-factor authentication, then it is a good idea to use it. You should definitely consider having it on anything that contains personal information or really sensitive information, like your banking account. But any time an account offers it, it is worth your time to use it as well.

DIFFERENT PASSWORDS ON ALL ACCOUNTS

Another lazy habit many of us can fall into is using the same password on more than one account. This is one thing if it is just an account that has nothing valuable like our Quora accounts. But if you have the same password on your banking accounts, your emails, and your social media profiles, think about how easy it would be for a hacker to gain all your information, and probably steal quite a bit of money in the process as well, especially if they just have to use the same username and passwords for all your account? And if the hacker gets one password, you can bet that they will try to see how many other websites they can access with that combination as well.

That is why it is important to go through and put different passwords and usernames for each of your accounts as possible. If you are running into some troubles remembering what all those passwords are, then consider a password manager. This can ensure that you utilize strong login information, even if they are complicated and complex to remember, and then you can pull out that password manager to fill it in and help you get things done. The harder the password, and the fewer times you reuse it, the safer your data will be against hackers and scammers.

NEVER STORE YOUR CARDS WITH ONLINE ACCOUNTS

If you must shop online, then don't fall into the bad habit of leaving your card information with the company you use. It may be a hassle, especially if you use that same company over and over again, but each time you go and make a purchase, take out the card and type in the number and other information again. This will make sure that the company is not being trusted with your card details and that no one else is able to access it.

Leaving your card information there may seem convenient and takes up less time and hassle on your part, but it is basically setting you up for hackers to get on and steal it. If there is a big data breach, the first thing the hackers will want is as many credit card numbers as possible. If yours is not stored in the website's database, then it is a bit harder for the hacker to get what they want.

If you must leave a card on file with an online storefront, only use a burner card from Privacy.com.

AVOID THE REWARDS PROGRAMS

Those rewards programs always look enticing and appear as if they are the best way to get something for pretty much nothing. And depending on which rewards program you go with, maybe it is a great deal. But remember that this is basically another way for a company to make a lot of money off of you, and with more than one method.

First, the company is making a lot of money by sending you deals based on your past buying habits. This is more likely to get you in the door and can make it so that you will purchase that item, and maybe a few more items to tempt you. So, they have just been able to entice you and get you in the door with the help of some good deals, and they make money on that.

Then there is a second way the company can make money, and this is the one you should be more worried about than the first. All that data they have collected on you, about your shopping habits and all the other things you do, can be very valuable to some marketers who want to know more about you. The company can sell all this information to those marketers, and they will make a significant amount of money from it in the process. This is a second way that they will make some money, and your information is then out there for anyone to see.

GET EVERYONE ON THE SAME PAGE

You can spend a lot of time working on the tips that we talk about in this chapter, and in all of the other chapters in this guidebook, but if there is someone on your network who is doing things wrong and isn't following the rules, then your information is still at risk. This is why you need to communicate with others in your family and make sure that all of you are on the same page, right from the beginning.

You can all sit down in a family meeting and decide which course of action is the best, discuss why you are taking these steps, and why everyone needs to follow them. You can even go through and discuss which rules will be followed. Everyone has to be on the same page and work together, or the companies will still be able to take your information or follow you around and sell your data to others, and there will be nothing you can do about it.

Keeping your identity safe and making sure no one is able to come through and take it from you will be so important as we work through all of this. And as you can see, there are quite a few steps you can take to prevent unauthorized users from getting onto your system or follow your every move. Even taking action on some concepts we discussed here will make a world of difference and can ensure you'll be able to keep what you want private and away from others.

THERE ARE MANY WAYS THAT COMPANIES AND SOCIAL MEDIA sites and online browsing can come together and learn a lot about us. This data collection is a big business, and it is not likely that companies are going to stop any time soon. And as more time goes on, they will likely come up with new and innovative ways to take your data, which we may not even be aware of yet.

There was a lot of information in this guidebook about the best practices and the best ways to keep your information safe and secure. We talked about limiting your social media sites, being careful with which search engines you choose to use, picking out the right hardware and software, and more. This is good news because it means there are a ton of options you can work with in order to keep the marketers out of your life while protecting your own personal information.

However, it was a lot to keep track of. You may have a list a mile long now about things you want to do to get your data safe, and you may feel like the only way to stay safe is to close your computers right now, and turn off your phones, and never use them again.

Data privacy and security is not about reaching perfection. It is impossible to go through and do everything on this list and maintain some sort of normalcy when it comes to the health of your personal data. It would be nice if the big names would just leave our data alone, but that is not going to happen either, as long as they can make money from us in the process. That doesn't mean that you need to go crazy, trying to do each and every step that we suggest in this guidebook. And we don't suggest it either.

The goal is to continually improve and to see results. Even changing just a handful of things about how you browse and do things online will make a world of difference. Getting rid of a few social media sites, changing your settings, and doing a few of the other tips and suggestions in this guidebook could keep many companies out of your data and could keep you safer.

Don't get stressed out because this seems too hard and you feel like you can never accomplish all of it. That is not the point of this guidebook. The point is to show you that it is possible to take your data and your privacy into your own hands and see some amazing results. Just start out slow, and continually work to add more things in, and learn more about what the big companies want when working with you, and then build up from there until you find something that seems to be the best mixture of fun online and safety for your personal information.

REFERENCES & LINKS:

For more information and to stay up-to-date with the latest information on Digital Privacy and online security, visit:

www.digitalprivacy.online

VPN Recommendations:

1. Proton VPN
2. NordVPN
3. Mullvad VPN
4. IPVN

Password Manager Recommendations:

1. BitWarden
2. Dash-lane
3. NordPass
4. KeePassXC
5. LessPass
6. Zoho Vault

Burner Credit Cards: Privacy.com

Internet Removal Service: DeleteMe

www.digitalprivacy.online